THE ART OF PLOTTING

THE ART OF PLOTTING

HOW TO ADD EMOTION, EXCITEMENT, AND DEPTH TO YOUR WRITING

Linda J. Cowgill

Back Stage Books
An imprint of Watson-Guptill Publications
New York

First published in 2008 by Back Stage Books,

an imprint of Watson-Guptill Publications, the Crown Publishing Group,

a division of Random House, Inc., New York

www.crownpublishing.com
www.watsonguptill.com

Library of Congress Control Number: 2007933739

ISBN-13: 978-1-58065-070-0

ISBN-10: 1-58065-070-8

First printing 2008

Printed in the United States of America

2 3 4 5 6 7 8 9/14 13 12 11 10 09

TO DAVID AND CLEA,

WHO MAKE EVERYTHING WORTHWHILE.

AND TO THE STUDENTS OVER THE YEARS

WHO HAVE HELPED ME DEFINE MY IDEAS.

Acknowledgments viii

Introduction x

Chapter 1 The Three Requirements of Drama 1

Chapter 2 Plot: Event and Emotion 9

So What Exactly Is Plot? 9

The Emotional Pattern of Plot 12

Great Movies Are Based on Strong, Simple Story Lines 17

Chapter 3 The Role of Conflict 23

At the Start: Conflict and Tension 24

Characters in Conflict 26

Meaningful Conflict 29

Unity of Opposites: Locking the Conflict 30

The Third Force: The Agent for Change 31

Emotional and Physical Conflict 35

Important Conflict vs. Big Conflict 36

Conflict Develops Positively *and* Negatively 37

The Importance of Failure to Your Protagonist's Character Arc 39

Chapter 4 The Principles of Action 41

Cause-and-Effect Scene Relationships 43

Rising Conflict 50

Foreshadowing Conflict 61

Chapter 5 The Tools of Plotting 65

Action Tools 66

Character Tools 74

Exposition Tools 87

Chapter 6 The Sequence of Story 95
The Outline of Events 97
Feature Films Are Structured in Groups of Scenes 98
Film Segments 106

Chapter 7 The Real Art of Plotting 113
Transforming Plot Points into Plotted Points 114
Deepening Our Characterizations along with Audience Involvement 119
Plotting for Emotion and Not Sentimentality 122
Preparations and Consequences 125
Plotting for Suspense 131
The Relationship between Anticipation and Surprise 140
The Obligatory Scene 143

Chapter 8 Common Problems in Plot Construction 147
Scripts Overplotted in Action 147
People Can't Relate—Why? 152
Understanding When the Audience Knows What 160
To-ing and Fro-ing: Using Too Many Beats to Accomplish the Task 162
The Passive Protagonist: Moving from Conflicted to Compelling 163

Chapter 9 Tools for Analysis 167
Discovering the Passive Protagonist 167
Identifying the Core Conflict to Serve as the Story Spine 169
Identifying Positive and Negative Scene Values 171
Identifying the Key Relationship the Audience Can Root For 172

Chapter 10 In the End 177
Referenced Films 180
Bibliography 182
Index 183
About the Author 184

ACKNOWLEDGMENTS

The Art of Plotting would not have been possible without the help of numerous people whom it is my pleasure to thank here.

Jeff Black at Hollywood Creative Directory, whose support and help have been always great and deeply appreciated.

Andy Shrader, for believing in the ideas and helping me get the seminar up and running.

Patrick Ulmstead, for making things easier.

Joe Byron, for support and inspiration.

Diana Derycz-Kessler, for the room to grow at the Los Angeles Film School.

Kathryn Galan at NALIP, the National Association of Latino Independent Producers, for giving me the opportunity to present *The Art of Plotting* to willing students.

Andrew Laskos, whose film discussions and vast movie knowledge were incredibly helpful.

Bill Bleich and Glen Benest, for their insightful critiques early on.

Gary Sunshine, whose sharp eye and attention to detail have helped my text immeasurably.

David DeCrane, for analysis, insight, and support. I could not have done it without you, nor would I have wanted to.

I have to thank my students at the Los Angeles Film School, and all over the world, who have appreciated my ideas and allowed me the honor to work with theirs.

"Every good idea and all creative work are
the offspring of the imagination,
and have their source in what
one is pleased to call infantile fantasy."

—C. G. Jung

INTRODUCTION

What is screenwriting?

A) An occupation

B) An art form

C) A disease

If you chose any of these answers, you'd be correct—and if you chose all three, you get extra credit. For many, screenwriting is both a delight and a curse. It's a creative outlet that affords writers the chance to allow their dreams to take shape. All too often, however, the realities and demands of the marketplace crush the pleasure of the process. Of course, there's no rule that says every good script must sell. But, frequently, a writer who believes his script has all the components of a great movie faces deep disappointment when his work fails to gather any interest because, in truth, the writer really had little understanding of the unique requirements of a *film* story.

Most of us are introduced to narrative writing when we compose essays and short stories in school. However rich our imaginations and compelling our prose, our work is judged as stories that are *read*, rather than as the blueprint for a story that will be *seen*. There is a major difference between the two types of writing. Screenwriting relies on the language of drama to communicate ideas effectively to the audience. Screenwriting utilizes an active voice as opposed to a passive one and requires action and conflict to develop meaning.

The Art of Plotting will help you understand this language of drama so that you can make your stories more satisfying to your first audience who is still a *reader*, but also a professional who is looking for stories that will make great movies. The goal is to excite this reader with effective *plotting*, which includes strong characterizations, story momentum, and tension. The art of plotting is all about how you lead your audience through the *information* of the story, keeping them intrigued and excited so they *feel* the way you want them to feel throughout the whole experience. As a screenwriter you are not just forcing them to ask, "What happens next?" You are managing their emotions at each stage of the story. The art of plotting is the art of transforming a dry narration of events into an emotional experience.

This book is not a beginner's manual. To get the most out of it, you'll need a basic knowledge of screenwriting. There is no formula I set forth that promises to turn you into a top-selling screenwriter. What *The Art of Plotting* offers is insight into key issues in plot design and construction: how you put your information together to make your story more powerful and important to your audience. I start by defining plot clearly and then show that plot is not only about creating a sequence of scenes that illustrates the events of the story but also about managing the resultant emotion. The aim is to give you tools that integrate plot, characterization, exposition, *and* emotion to create stories that are compelling and meaningful.

Since Syd Field's *Screenplay* hit the racks twenty-five years ago, the number of screenwriting books has multiplied exponentially. The focus of most of these texts has been on structure—how to build the relationship between the parts that hold the whole work together. But even with all this attention to plot points, premise techniques, and dramatic building blocks, many of the most sharply chiseled three-act stories fall flat. Emotion is what's missing.

Now more books and teachers are finally talking specifically about this elusive ingredient. Emotion, however, has always been a part of the screenwriting lexicon; it just hasn't been explained well. It's the hardest part of screenwriting to teach because it's more difficult to quantify than action, obstacles, and complications. To play emotion effectively, you need an understanding of human nature, if not fundamental psychology. The luckiest students have picked it up almost intuitively and incorporated it in their work. But if you read Aristotle, Lajos Egri, or John Howard Lawson, you'll see they all talk about "emotion," though in different ways. Aristotle talks about catharsis, amplitude, pity, and fear. Egri speaks of the progression of character in terms of emotions. Lawson writes about dramatic action within a social framework. They just don't explain how to show it.

Don't think I'm throwing out the importance of structure. I wrote an entire book on the topic—*Secrets of Screenplay Structure*. You have to have structure and truly understand how it works to create a story that has maximum emotional effect. But good structure alone is not what makes a story powerful.

There are three main areas I discuss here. The first is this idea of emotion. It doesn't matter if you get to an emotional payoff with laughter, fear, or tears (or all three), but you have to get there. Many writers are afraid of emotion and leave it out entirely; or they rely on easily stereotyped emotions such as sadness or anger. A successful screenplay must be conceived both in terms of plot action and emotion. A writer needs to know what he wants his reader to *feel* while judging his screenplay, and it's the plot line that is his only tool.

Second, many screenwriters overplot their stories with too much action and event, constructing their screenplays in a long list of separate scenes, sixty or so, and expecting readers to follow along and get the point of each. Your audience won't be able to track a story that has an original point in every single scene. You're writing drama, not a novel; you can't stop the narrative to explain every nuance. The plots of movies develop in segments, groups of scenes expanding a main idea that then advances the plot. You don't want to overload the plot with incident after incident. This propensity leads to an important, underappreciated law of screenwriting: *When you overplot in terms of action, you underplot in terms of character and emotion.* You won't have time to work in illustrative character responses to the conflict when your plot depends on a lot of action.

Third, writing a script has as much to do with understanding the technique of writing for film as it does with action or inspiration. I cover in detail the technical issues of assembling the scenes and sequences of your plot to get the most dramatic bang out of your ideas. I examine the role conflict plays in creating a great plot, how to increase tension and suspense, and the ways to deepen your characterizations along with the audience's involvement in your story. I show you how to transform plot points into active beats of storytelling as well as how to recognize and overcome the most common plotting problems.

The overall goal of this book is to help you understand the principles of action and plotting in a way that will give you another set of tools to use when you look at your own work. With these tools, you'll be able to deepen the emotional impact of the conflict on the characters, simplify your story lines so that the action flows better, and tell the story you want to tell.

I often ask my students, which is more important, plot or character? There is always controversy, and opposing sides will often cite the same movies to make their points. When that happens it's very revealing because in a great movie the two *are* inseparable—plot is character and character is plot. It mirrors what the Greek philosopher Heraclitus said: A man's character is his fate (that is, the "plot" of his life). We could just as easily reverse this idea and say a man's fate is his character. *The Art of Plotting* demonstrates this.

CHAPTER 1

THE THREE REQUIREMENTS OF DRAMA

INT. STUDY - NIGHT

As rain lashes the window, the young writer sits at her desk before her computer and excitedly opens the book to the first page. About to read the opening sentence, a LOUD KNOCK at the door interrupts her. She frowns, but keeps reading. The KNOCKING persists. She glances up, pausing to consider the door.

Screenwriting is the art of putting words on paper to create visual images in the mind of a reader that excite and impress him. You lead him through the corridors of your imagination to express your dreams. You build characters with actions and dialogue. You strive to convey interesting revelations. You choose your words carefully to create just the right impression. But in the end, if you can't produce a plot that grabs the reader and keeps him turning pages, it won't matter how beautifully you write or how wonderful your imagery; you won't sell.

There's a common misconception about screenwriting that

writing the script is simply telling a story in scenes with dialogue and action. But this is far from the truth. For a film to work, information has to be conveyed in such a way that the audience tracks it visually and audibly and so that they're interested in what's happening. They must be able to understand it with eyes and ears as they watch the scenes unfold.

Every day writers start screenplays that are misconceived and doomed because they don't understand the underlying principles of drama. They believe assembling a string of incidents—a character does this and goes here, then meets another character, and something else happens—will somehow create a dramatic story. This may be the case in writing a short story or novel because incidents can be shaped and framed by the author's voice in the narrative. But even in films in which narration is employed as a storytelling device, drama requires more than the sum of a number of incidents.

Because this book isn't a complete manual for everything you need to know about screenwriting, but is focused on the art of plotting, it doesn't cover the basics beyond defining plot. You should have a fundamental understanding of story structure in film to fully appreciate the ideas presented here. A look at any of a great number of good books on the topic will provide you with this foundation. But let me just say this: Plot structure can be viewed as a two-part process. First is the overall form the story takes. Second is the actual plotting of the scenes, the order and arrangement of specific events and details that create specific meanings. The overall structure focuses on the relationships between beginnings and endings, on the development of conflicts in the middle, and how these parts hold the elements of your story together. Plotting finds the connections in the specific scenes and sequences.

The ultimate plot structure of a story depends on many things: genre, your point of view, even your true purpose for writing it.

These particular considerations contribute to making your work unique. But even as you strive for originality, you must realize that good structure tends to follow basic rules. The beginning of a film must set up a dramatic problem for the protagonist (act one). The middle builds the story's rising action (act two), which then intensifies to the final climax and resolution (in act three). This "formula" is simple enough in theory, but in practice, keeping the characters on track, the story moving ahead, the theme meaningful, and the audience from becoming bored can be an infuriatingly difficult task.

Without an intensive review, I'll boil the art of screenwriting down to three essential ingredients, what I call the Three Requirements of Drama. Everything in this book is predicated on these three ideas:

- We must have a character, the protagonist, who will take action to achieve something.
- The protagonist must meet with conflict.
- When it's all over, the story must mean something.

These ideas may seem too simple to form the basis of screenwriting. Surely, there must be more. And of course there is—much more. But experience has taught me that many new and intermediate screenwriters, and even some successful ones who craft complete misses, either don't entirely understand these principles or flat out reject them, and so they spend large amounts of time and effort writing scripts that will never work. Before we begin, let's review these ideas carefully so that we understand their application to this fine art.

1. The protagonist must act. Every screenwriting book worth its cover price says this; therefore, there must be something to it. However, most books present this gem as a given, like a prime number or the law of gravity. It just is. Let's understand why.

Drama needs characters who desire, who want, who need, and

who will act (even if the action is reactive, or centered on the avoidance of action) for two reasons. First, it provides a clear framework for the audience that is viewing the film to understand the flow of events. This is the initial way they plug into the story and get oriented. What is the protagonist doing? What does she want? Will she achieve her goals? This raises the dramatic question of plot. Will Dorothy find her way home in *The Wizard of Oz*? In *Stranger than Fiction,* can Harold Crick locate the author who intends to kill his character in her book?

Second, desire creates the driving force for the action. It compels the character to move toward something, and this builds the first part of the forward momentum that keeps a great film from feeling static. Whether the character's goal is the same from start to finish (*Kill Bill, Vol. 1* and *Vol. 2*), or part of a series of steps to accomplish something (*The Shawshank Redemption*), the action supplies the cohesion for a sequence of scenes. If characters simply meander from scene to scene, with no clear goals or prospects, after a while (and sooner rather than later, unless we're seeing something hilariously funny) we lose interest because the characters seem to be heading nowhere and we can't understand the connections between the actions enough to assign basic meaning.

2. The protagonist must meet with *conflict*. There must be trouble, opposition, problems for a protagonist to face. Conflict can be subtle or overt, but it must be apparent. Conflict's necessary because it builds the tension that keeps the audience interested in what happens next. It does much more than this, but this is its starting point. The audience must understand where conflict comes from and why it's happening. We'll discuss conflict in depth in a later chapter. But know that this creation of tension activates in your audience an instinctive desire to see conflict resolved. Can the protagonist overcome the conflict? Or will the

conflict overcome him? If your protagonist simply walks around, making discoveries and solving puzzles, the intellectual curiosity can hold the viewer for a while, but eventually your audience's interest will wane and you'll lose them.

These two ideas, desire and conflict, work together to create a context for the story's information so an audience that is *seeing and hearing* a film instead of *reading a script or novel* will understand what's going on. This is the key point. The audience is *viewing*, not reading. This is a completely different mode of understanding. Reading is an active activity while viewing is a passive one. The reader actively reads the words on paper, making the decision to keep turning pages or not. Stories can be picked up and read at will while films play out in specific duration (though DVD viewing may eventually alter how we watch drama). With film, viewers sit and watch as action happens, and screenwriters have to work harder to hold their interest with the on-screen activity. With a book, the voice of the narrator can lead readers through the material, making leaps and connections by way of what is really a commentary on the action. Tension and meaning can be created by what the writer tells the readers. And if readers don't understand a passage, they can reread it until they do. But in film, the action must develop in a way that is clearly understood as it happens and builds tension so the audience stays involved. On the most superficial level, every story is about the quest to attain a goal and whether a character will achieve it. Conflict casts doubt on the character's ultimate success and increases our interest.

Film, as with theater and music, is a temporal art form. It communicates its content within a precise time span. The audience must be able to process the information and make meaningful connections to understand it. Drama drives home its information differently than narrative prose. In a book, an author can make explicit a character's thoughts. In film, especially if voiceover narration isn't used, screenwriters must externalize what characters feel and think, and this can be extremely difficult. Screenwriters use specific actions growing out of characters' wants and needs—their objectives—to keep the audience clued in to the plot. As film has become more naturalistic, it has left behind most theatrical conventions such as asides, monologues, and the chorus and relies on true-to-life behavior to convey the sense of realism the audience expects.

3. When it's all over, the story must mean something. Narrative films need action and conflict to frame the important ideas the writer is concerned with and make them compelling to the audience. At the first level, we understand the story in terms of what the character is doing in the face of the conflict. Does she succeed or fail? Viewers need to grasp the nature of the conflict, where it originates, how it develops and affects the characters, and how and why it resolves the way it does, for the story to make sense and satisfy them. Sometimes this is all the meaning we need. There is no "moral to the tale," so to speak. Many great Looney Tunes demonstrate just this, and many fun films, too.

If, however, the writer pays enough attention to these questions to answer them truthfully, she winds up developing a real theme. This goes to the heart of what this book is about. Meaning is developed through how the conflict affects the characters, physically and emotionally. Real dramatic conflict is life changing. A great story details that change in a character and his circumstances and shows us why it comes about. *Witness* tells the story of an honest cop who is chased by bad cops and has to take refuge among the nonviolent Amish in Pennsylvania. That's the basic plot line and conflict. The premise of the film concerns the place of violence in American society and what it does to those who live with it. *Casablanca* is the story of what happens when a cynical ex-patriot encounters the old flame who caused his bitterness. Its theme explores the selflessness of true love.

You don't have to be profound to create a theme. But you do have to tell the truth. Meaning comes from characters reacting truthfully in a situation. What's new and profound about *The Departed*? It's basically about how crime doesn't pay and justice will be served. But it's a well-crafted and interesting take on an old chestnut that's been visited time and time again.

The three requirements of drama are your starting point in screenwriting. Every idea for a film can be evaluated in these terms. The active protagonist who encounters a conflict and develops our understanding of the problem will ground a story in action, tension, and emotion, the very basis of the language of drama.

CHAPTER 2

PLOT: EVENT AND EMOTION

For most people, the terms *story* and *plot* are synonymous. People read a book or go to a movie and come away saying, "What a great story!" But the reason the book or film is so affecting is generally because the story has a great plot. (Don't think I'm forgetting about character and its importance to a great story. I'm including it in plot as part of a well-told story.)

SO WHAT EXACTLY IS PLOT?

In literature or drama, plot encompasses three important factors.

Arrangement of Events

Plot refers to how events are arranged to achieve an intended effect. (One of Webster's definitions of *plot* is "a plan or scheme to accomplish a purpose.") A plot is constructed to make a point, to reach a climax that produces a specific result. All great plots are focused on where they're going to end up at the final climax and resolution.

Causality

Plot is not just A happens, B happens, and C happens. It's A happens and causes B to result, which in turn causes C, and so on. It isn't a timeline of events that just takes place. It is a structural imperative of dramatic storytelling. The cause-and-effect relationships between scenes push the story action forward as well as ensure that we understand the fundamental meaning of the action because we can see the connections *between* the scenes. We don't just see *what* is happening, but also *why*.

Causality applies to both linear and nonlinear plot construction. (By *nonlinear* we mean films such as *Citizen Kane*, *Pulp Fiction*, *Annie Hall*, *Rashômon*—stories in which the sequence of events does not follow chronologically.) In nonlinear films, the traditional use of time is broken, and scenes that would take place sequentially are positioned out of order. But these scenes are not just randomly placed. They must be linked with cause-and-effect relationships in sequences that allow the audience to understand and follow the plot. We see linearly plotted sequences in a nonlinear film that build the dramatic point at a specific juncture in the story and then climax and move into the next sequence in another time.

These cause-and-effect scene relationships develop the conflict and characterizations by illustrating the consequences of events and the decisions and choices that result because of them. In this vein, the adage "character is plot" or "character is fate" proves true. A well-defined character's personality inexorably demands a specific resolution, one that at the end of the story feels retrospectively inevitable. Great works of dramatic art achieve this feeling of inevitability with regard to *all* the major dramatis personae. Consider the fate of the major characters in stories such as *Dangerous Liaisons* or *Reflections in a Golden Eye*. Individually they feel psychologically real, and, when meshed together, the climax feels preordained.

Conflict

Dramatic conflict is the struggle that grows out of the interplay of opposing forces (ideas, interests, wills). Conflict creates tension and that awakens the audience's instinctive desire to watch other people fight it out: We want to satisfy the intellectual curiosity of knowing who wins or loses and to enjoy the accompanying feelings of satisfaction, joy, and/or schadenfreude. But while we are vicariously absorbed in the fight, we also want to understand the nature of the conflict, so our minds try to make sense of it. In the end, how we understand the resolution of the conflict is what makes for a satisfying conclusion.

We might say this: Plot is a series of interrelated actions that progresses through a struggle of opposing forces to a climax and resolution that define the meaning of the work. As fundamental as this is, many writers forget these basic concepts when writing and show the reader different aspects of the characters' lives or the events, moving from incident to incident as if on a timeline, and not linking actions together or finding the heart of the conflict. But these factors—the arrangement of events, causality, and conflict—contribute to how the audience tracks the events so that the story makes sense as it builds in momentum and tension to the climax.

Plot is really the management of information to make a story more involving and satisfying for an audience. Ten people can use the same source material, but only one writer will come up with *Oedipus Rex* or *Hamlet*. When you simply tell a story, you don't always make use of the factors I mentioned above. But when you *plot* a story, you are using them every step of the way.

THE EMOTIONAL PATTERN OF PLOT

The reason most of us go the movies is because films arouse our emotions. Generally, we don't go for intellectual ideas; we go for the excitement, suspense, the laughs, and the tears. Yet as we write, creating emotional material is often the most difficult part. We write around it or hit it right on the nose. Either way, it's not very effective. Also, many screenwriting books come right out and tell the writer emotion should be left to actors and directors and off the page. Consequently, scripts are written with a lot of action but very little feeling.

Emotion is the source of our connection with other people. We see someone in pain, and his suffering elicits our sympathy. We watch people celebrating, and their joy makes us smile. Emotion is the great universal that unites us all in the human condition. When we relate to people emotionally we often transcend racial, ethnic, and cultural differences. Our expression of emotion often conveys more about ourselves than all the words we can muster to explain who we are.

In *The Elements of Screenwriting*, Irwin Blacker wrote, "Plot is more than a pattern of events; it is the ordering of emotions." He understood that stories are as much about emotion as about plot action. Emotion makes movies compelling. Through the emotional reactions of the characters, we're drawn deeper into the story. A character's emotional life helps the audience to identify with the character and understand his motivations. It makes a character seem authentic and heightens the stakes by showing what's important to him, as well as communicating through these reactions what the story is really about.

When the emotional component of a story is left out, characters seem flat and unreal. We're given melodrama, where a story is all about the action and conflict, and we're never really shown the effect of that conflict on the characters except in the broadest of terms. Because we don't see this effect, the characters seem like puppets, moving at the puppet master's whim, and not like real people. Great writers understand that when they reveal characters' emotions, they reach the audience emotionally.

Plot: The Ordering of Actions and *Emotions*

When we think about plot we usually think in terms of action and conflict. The action is driven by what the characters want, and conflict stands in their way. These basic parameters give a plot direction and meaning: Characters act on their desires, their wants, which leads to action, which in turn leads to conflict.

But drama is as much about the repercussions of action as it is about the action itself. It's not just the action that frames the story but how characters respond to the action that ultimately conveys meaning to the audience. Is a character devastated when his lover rejects him, or secretly relieved? After arguing with his wife, does the protagonist unload his anger on his daughter and feel bad about it or just go get drunk? Different outcomes lend different interpretations to the material. And the more emotional the effect is, the more it often communicates to the audience, also allowing them to connect more deeply with the story. The audience needs to see the results of action and conflict—the consequences—to fully understand the dramatic weight that action carries. The emotional reaction to action is often where the heart of a drama lies.

Writers often write scenes that show us a character in conflict but not the result of that specific conflict, so we don't grasp the full meaning of it. For example, a screenwriter might create a scene in which the protagonist's girlfriend leaves him. He says he loves her, but she still goes. In the next scene, the hero sits in a coffee shop reading papers from work. In the next scene he has dinner with his friends. Now how do we understand the break-up? What does this second scene tell us? Does he care what happened? Maybe the specific reason for not showing his emotional reaction is to emphasize that the hero has problems with his feelings, and the reaction will come in a couple of scenes. But if it never comes, we can only understand that this action had no real effect on him and he didn't love her. I remember sitting with a writer who had written just such a sequence and asking how the hero felt about his girlfriend leaving. She told me the character was devastated. But how would I know that if I didn't see, on paper, the emotional fallout?

Writers are often fearful of putting in scenes that show an emotional response, thinking it will hold back the plot's momentum. Screenwriting teachers and books admonish writers not to put in emotional cues. But without these cues and scenes, the reader, and then the viewer, will never fully understand what the conflict means to the hero and the other important characters.

So plotting a story is more than just mapping out specific steps a character takes toward his goal within a conflict. Remember our definition of plot: It's the structuring of action *and* reaction (the emotion) to achieve an intended effect. We don't want emotion just for the sake of emotion; we need it to be related specifically to the actions and reactions of the characters involved in their specific struggle.

In the best movies, there's a pattern to the development, a progression of emotion that builds through the plot. Just as scenes must be plotted through action and reaction to convey the fundamental meaning as well as movement of the story, emotion must move in the same way. Characters' emotional reactions can't jump along from one polarized affect to another. For example, say your protagonist has an argument with her boss that could jeopardize her career. She leaves the scene feeling angry. In the next scene, you show her clowning around with friends. The jump from one emotion to its opposite will jar the audience because they haven't seen the reason for the change in attitude. The jump takes the audience out of the picture, so to speak, because they wonder what brought the change on. These reactions must be orchestrated in such a way that we see either the cause of the emotional change or the progression of emotion to understand the full meaning of the plot action.

Good stories are conflict driven; protagonists must fight their way through plots they are responsible for having set in motion. The harder the protagonist falls along the way, the more emotionally charged the story. Great writers rake their heroes over the coals because this is how stories develop emotion, and emotion is how stories connect with their audience.

The best plots incorporate the main characters' emotional reactions into the plot action to illustrate who they are as well as how these reactions drive the story. Think of the scene in *Jerry Maguire* when Jerry (Tom Cruise) is confronted by the son of his hockey-playing client, whose dad has just suffered his fourth concussion. The boy wants Jerry to get his dad to quit. Jerry gives the kid a glib response. The boy seethes; then says, "Fuck you." What does Jerry's reaction tell us about him? How does it set in motion the rest of the action that follows?

What about Schindler (Liam Neeson) at the end of *Schindler's List*, when he reveals his guilt over not doing more to save others? Or take our example above: the husband who argues with his wife and then dumps on his daughter. At the beginning of *American Beauty*, Lester (Kevin Spacey) has words with Carolyn (Annette Benning) after being brushed off by his daughter, Jane (Thora Birch), at the dinner table. He follows his daughter into the kitchen and tries to connect to her but winds up arguing with her instead. Screenwriter Alan Ball and director Sam Mendes show us their encounter without words. We see it through the lens of Ricky's (Wes Bentley) video camera as he watches through the kitchen window. We see words exchanged, and then Jane storms out. Then we watch as Lester sags at the sink, clearly regretting what's happened, and we know he feels bad. Just in case we don't know we're supposed to empathize with him, the filmmakers show us Ricky lower the camera, reacting to what he's just witnessed between father and daughter, moved and saddened.

What do these reactions tell us about the characters? In each one we glimpse a character at his core. The scenes give us more than an explanation that's contained in a background story; we understand their fundamental emotional depths and true characters through how they react. We see who they are, not in their stories they tell, but in the actions and reactions that define them.

When a character responds to dramatic events intensely (even if he represses or sublimates his response in, say, alcohol or misplaced anger), the audience sees what's important to him. People generally become emotional about the things that are most significant to them. The character's emotional response to conflict clues us in to who the character really is—even more than our character's original desire-fueled action. Which tells us more about Jim Carrey's character in *Bruce Almighty*: his original use of almighty power or the way he comes to regret the responsibilities that go with it?

When we think of the first *Jaws*, we remember the tension and scares. There is no comparison between the sequels and the original film. One of the reasons the first works so well, and the others don't, is because of its attention to how the conflict affects the characters.

Toward the end of the first act of *Jaws*, Chief Brody (Roy Scheider) thinks, along with everyone else but Hooper (Richard Dreyfuss), that the marauding shark has been caught. It hangs on the dock for all to see. Brody is happy, the mayor (Murray Hamilton) is happy, the whole town is happy. Then Mrs. Kintner (Lee Fierro) arrives and confronts Brody over the death of her son. As we watch the scene, we see the chief take responsibility for the death, even though we know he fought hard to close the beaches, and against the mayor and town interests. In the scene that follows at home, we see the effect that this confrontation has had on him—he can't eat, he's drinking and lost in his own thoughts—and we feel bad with him. Then we see his youngest son Sean mimicking the chief's posture and gestures, quietly trying to gain his father's attention. Brody notices him, too. He responds by gently acknowledging his son through the boy's game. In the end, he leans close to Sean and says, "Give us a kiss." "Why?" Sean asks. "Because I need it." The interaction with his son humanizes him. In spite of his emotional pain, he can still relate with Sean, and this helps us to care about him even more.

The best writers understand and use this type of plotting, cause- and emotion-laden effect, to make the audience care more about their stories. They find the balance between event and consequence that allows us to relate to the characters and they are able to weave the tapestry of action and emotion, the elements of plot and character, to tell page-turning stories.

GREAT MOVIES ARE BASED ON STRONG, SIMPLE STORY LINES

What separates most professional screenplays that get made into successful movies from amateurs' scripts? The professionals' scripts are based on strong simple story lines that are well developed in terms of action, conflict, and character and the effect of the conflict on the characters. As a result, these scripts feel complex and genuine. Characters seem authentic, with emotional lives, and the action has weight and meaning.

Amateur scripts are *over*plotted in terms of action and *under*plotted in terms of character and emotion. We see lots of scenes with the characters running from one problem to the next, getting in and out of scraps, but we don't see the effect of the conflict on those characters. The result is the amateur screenplays feel confused and flat. Ultimately, meaning is sacrificed, and the reader is left not knowing what to feel.

Take a good look at a great movie and you'll see at its core a clear strong action line that everything else revolves around. In *American Beauty*, Lester's action starts when he sees Angela (Mena Suvari) at the basketball game and his fantasy engages. His desire for her threatens everything in his life—his marriage, his relationship with his daughter, even his freedom (if Angela's underage). Although Lester doesn't overtly pursue her at the start, she wakes him up and he responds by changing, and this affects his wife and daughter, resulting in actions that show the audience who these characters are and push the plot forward. Everything starts from here and intersects with this through-line, through *obstacles* and *complications* (see Chapter 5, "Action Tools," for definitions), incorporating the characters' reactions to the conflict that motivate further actions.

In great movies, characters are defined by their specific goals *and* their emotional reactions. Screenwriters set characters up at the top of the script with specific traits and emotional lives. At the beginning of *Shakespeare in Love*, Will starts the story frustrated and blocked. He owes his producer a play, but he can't get beyond the title. At the start of *American Beauty,* Lester, too, is frustrated, but even more: He hates his life. As the characters face their conflicts through the course of the action, some things go right and others wrong. How the characters react to these differing outcomes gives the audience insight into who each one is.

Once the setup is complete, emotion progresses through the story in relation to the protagonist's goals, the conflict, and/or other characters. Emotional reactions intensify as conflict escalates and the climax approaches. By the end of the plot, when the character arrives at the climax, the encounter with the main conflict has changed him and/or the world around him. We understand this change through the emotion surrounding it. In *Shakespeare in Love* and *American Beauty*, both Will and Lester have grown through their ordeals. Will has finally experienced a true love and become a man; Lester has rediscovered his humanity and found himself. Both climaxes are shaded by a new emotional state for each character.

Erin Brockovich is an interesting example. At the end of the movie it doesn't appear Erin (Julia Roberts) has really changed. Her circumstances have, but at first viewing she seems like a protagonist who forces the people around her to change while she herself stays the same. If we dig a little deeper, however, we find Erin *does* change, through the force of her emotions.

Let's take a look.

In act one, Erin is desperate, angry, defensive, and alienated. She feels like a victim and doesn't like it. She's angry about her life and how it's turned out. Specific scenes show us her pain and anger. The movie starts with her job interview. This shows us what she wants: a job. She doesn't get it. The filmmakers take a long beat on Erin standing outside smoking, leaning on the wall, before she gets in her car, only to be hit in an intersection. In these few scenes we see she's angry and hurt, and we feel her frustration and desperation. When she sues the ER doctor who hit her and loses her case, we feel it even more deeply.

We also see qualities: her sacrifice for her children when she feeds them in the restaurant and orders nothing for herself; her determination to find a job—which ultimately leads her back to her lawyer, Ed Masry (Albert Finney). Ed hears her desperation and gives her a chance. She takes it seriously and works hard. We see glimpses of her compassion, but she's still gruff, angry, defensive, and alienated in the office. Eventually, she loses her job because she doesn't understand how to work in the world.

In act two, Erin is vulnerable and depressed as well as angry, defensive, and alienated. But this represents an emotional change, a change in her character: Because she is vulnerable, she allows George (Aaron Eckhart) into her life. This is a positive step, although it could lead to disaster, too (given who he is on the surface).

When ex-boss Ed comes back to Erin with a question about a case, Erin shrewdly gets her job back. She returns to work but is still angry. She hears stories on the job that stir her compassion, but she remains defensive at home and unable to deal with her angry son.

Pressure mounts as she sees the enormity of the wrong done to the people of Hinkley, California. Upset and angry, she forces Ed to listen to her. This moves the case to a higher level. Part of Erin's problem is that her anger works for and against her. Her anger helps her in this specific job by keeping her focused on the company that has victimized the town residents. But the anger is destructive when brought home, where it drives a wedge between her and her son, and George.

Her work pays off, however, and Erin wins over more people to make the Jensen case a class-action suit. Now Erin feels more confident. The big attorneys, Kurt and Theresa (Peter Coyote and Veanne Cox), come onto the case, and this threatens Erin. Defensive, she goes too far and insults Theresa in front of everyone. Now Ed gets angry, and he shames Erin over her behavior. Erin is forced to the sidelines while the big guns do their stuff, but she's not happy about it, although it gives her time to think.

But in act three, because the townspeople can't relate to the big lawyers, the case starts falling apart. "This case needs you,"

Ed tells Erin. She gets the case back on track and, validated, she's now able to apologize and ask George for help and to make headway with her son.

At the end of Erin and Ed's campaign to sign everyone up, Erin meets a strange man, Charles Embry (Tracey Walter), in a bar. Because her attitude has now changed, she doesn't immediately blow him off. Good thing, too, because he has the documents that prove corporate PG&E is accountable.

Erin Brockovich has more emotional moments than those noted here. Many scenes are marked with emotionally charged reactions that help us understand Erin and feel for and with her, from minor moments like getting a parking ticket to a heart-clenching encounter with a child dying of cancer. Throughout the film emotion intensifies the drama, raises the stakes, and generally expresses and confirms a psychological growth pattern in Erin's behavior.

Successful screenwriters use emotional responses to conflict to define who their characters are. Setting up the conflict, the roadblocks on the hero's path, is obviously a necessary task. Equally important, however, is illustrating your hero's emotional reaction to these roadblocks. Don't be in a hurry to get your protagonist over the next hurdle. Instead, take a moment, or scene, or sequence, and show how unexpected hurdles and setbacks affect your character emotionally, and force him to confront himself. If you take the time and do that, the next bump in the road might, with a different emotional mindset, turn out to be something your hero sees as a launching pad to his goal.

CHAPTER 3

THE ROLE OF CONFLICT

Recently, I had an enlightening experience while working out a new exercise on conflict and desires. I decided to find a scene from a great movie, about a page long, and alter the names and omit the action, limiting the text only to the dialogue. The idea was to look at the scene stripped of the description of the action (conflict and desire) to see how the presence of these elements made the scene stronger and more interesting.

To my surprise, in every scene I found at this length (and longer), even stripped of the action and direction, conflict and desire were so strongly linked to the flow of the ideas that they informed the development of the dialogue and the scene. In that evening of digging through dozens of scripts, I saw clearly what great writers know: These two elements—action (characters wanting) and conflict (the obstacles and complications)—create momentum, interest, and drama in scenes that hold our attention and live in our memories.

Many writers don't truly understand what conflict means to their stories, so they don't use it effectively. They either dissipate the tension by relegating the conflict to the background or pump it up gratuitously in meaningless violence. Conflict isn't some arbitrary device used simply to create tension to hook the audience. It is an essential ingredient for a great film. Action in drama and fiction depends on conflict. Without it, a story sits on the page (or screen), static and immobile. The audience (readers or viewers) goes along for a little while out of curiosity but finally gives up because the story hasn't kept their attention. Without conflict, characters may act, but they never truly reveal themselves. A film might be about the selflessness of true love, but unless its characters face a strong conflict, the audience isn't really going to care.

AT THE START: CONFLICT AND TENSION

Let's begin by discussing how the conflict behind a story is conceived and formulated, because this is where so many screenplays start to go awry. And if they go amiss here, it's pretty hard to get them back on track. Often conflict is set up as trouble to be overcome between characters—the protagonist and antagonist. In other cases, conflict is based in a predicament the protagonist encounters. Obviously, this is the starting point from which to *develop* the main conflict. But it doesn't go far enough. A conflict's evolution and consequences serve to define characters and themes—as well as hold the audience's interest, as discussed in the last chapter.

From the outset, conflict must be clear to the writer. You must understand not only the dramatic question that's raised in the main conflict but also the obstacles, both outer and inner, and the complications that the protagonist and other characters face in the plot. The problems must truly be difficult for the protagonist, making the audience uncertain about his success as well as fear his failure. A strong conflict leaves the audience worried by the real danger threatening the characters yet still hopeful everything will turn out all right in the end.

When there is no hope, the audience can only feel despair, and this is something to consider carefully. Without hope, your audience often starts closing off, defending hearts and minds against the tragic onslaught. It makes it harder to reach them emotionally. The film *The House of Sand and Fog*, from the critically acclaimed book by Andre Dubus III, is nearly unrelenting in the tragic circumstances surrounding all the characters, which may be the main reason moviegoers didn't connect with it. By the time the tragedy hits, the audience had already walled themselves off protectively. In the best tragedies there are always comic moments amidst all the conflict. These humorous beats allow us to relax our guard, so that when the devastating moment arrives, it packs a real punch. Think of how powerful the climax is in *One Flew over the Cuckoo's Nest*. The comedy has completely defused our protective natures. Even *Se7en* has two real laughs in it, to help the audience cope with the extreme tension.

It's not simply conflict—the clash of opposing forces—that creates the tension that keeps the audience watching; often it's the anticipation of the coming conflict and its unforeseeable outcome that strains their emotional equilibrium. There are four basic forms of dramatic tension a writer uses to plot a story, and it's important to understand how they function for the audience. Each one creates natural anxiety and anticipation regarding future events. They are the tension of the task, the tension of relationships, the tension of mystery, and the tension of surprise.

The *tension of the task* makes us ask, Will the protagonist's goals be accomplished? Can he succeed or not? Conflict in the form of obstacles and complications threatens the protagonist with failure.

The *tension of relationships* comes from us wondering how these connections will be affected by the difficulties the protagonist and other characters encounter. Inherently, most people want to see the protagonist connect with another character in an important way. Will these bonds maintain and get stronger or deteriorate in the face of conflict?

The *tension of mystery* rests in our need to have puzzles solved. We want answers, to be able to understand how and why things happen as well as what will happen.

The *tension of surprise* develops when the action doesn't go as we expected, startling us, and now making us anticipate other possibilities.

Understanding these four basic tensions allows the writer to maximize conflict and deepen the audience's interest and connection with her work. From these tensions emerges one that serves as the main conflict of the film. The other problems are plotted around it. In films with situational conflicts in this position, like *Little Children* and *Touching the Void*, the protagonists collide with their circumstances and environment, sometimes represented by other characters, and sometimes not. In films like *Stranger than Fiction* and *The Wizard of Oz*, the protagonists clash with main antagonists. Whichever this through-line is based on, it will define the parameters of the plot, indicating what needs to be set up in the beginning and what must be resolved at the end.

CHARACTERS IN CONFLICT

When we analyze a great movie, we see a simplicity in the juxtaposition of its main oppositions. The characters (specifically in the protagonist/antagonist axis, but in other character relationships, too) aren't generally just people on different sides of a problem. Most of the time they are rival characters used to contrast each other. One character is "good" and the other is "evil."

This is, of course, simplistic, but consider Luke Skywalker and Darth Vader: Luke represents the good and Vader, the bad. One has the dominant positive value and the other the negative. (The use of other characters in *Star Wars IV: A New Hope* also helps to delineate these opposites. Contrast the opportunist Han Solo with Luke and Vader; although not as power driven as Vader or as idealistic as Luke, Han defines himself as a "stand-up guy" when he returns to help the resistance at the climax of the movie.)

Opposing characters aren't understood solely as antagonists, however; they represent opposing ideas. They make the issue of the story clearer and the meaning more easily grasped because the characters are revealed in their opposing traits and values. They may have similarities, but there will be fundamental differences, too, and these differences define the true nature of the conflict.

In *The Break-Up*, Gary (Vince Vaughn) and Brooke (Jennifer Aniston) are opposites just because one's a man and the other's a woman, and this is the fundamental way the story is to be understood. Fun-loving Gary is the archetypal male who has never grown up—immature, narcissistic, and insensitive. He's used to getting his way and having things done for him. Brooke is the reliable female, ready to shoulder running the home but winding up resenting Gary when he just won't help with daily household responsibilities. When she reaches her limit and explodes, breaking up with him, Gary reacts and digs his heels in. He goes into power mode and takes the offensive, trying to drive her out of the condo to keep the spoils of their relationship for himself. Brooke, on the other hand, still wants Gary, but she wants him to change and value what they have together. This is the basic conflict: Can Brooke make Gary change and grow up? The story isn't just about "men and women" per se. Ultimately, it's about maturity and responsibility in relationships. It's shown in the contrast of the immature male and the more responsible female who loves but conflicts with him.

In *Se7en*, Somerset (Morgan Freeman) is a man who respects life even though he may want to withdraw from the disturbing world around him. But he could never so viciously attack it as the serial killer John Doe does. Somerset is thoughtful, meticulous, and constant. He's contrasted with his hotheaded partner, Mills (Brad Pitt), who is ruled by his emotions, easily frustrated and quick to act. The villain, John Doe (Kevin Spacey), is fundamentally opposed to Somerset. He may share Somerset's worldview, but his sadistic drive to annihilate and destroy defines his misanthropy and his negative value.

In *American Beauty*, the main conflict for Lester is with his wife, Carolyn. Their marriage isn't working and both are unhappy, but only Lester is willing to admit it. The other engages in covert marital warfare. Their opposition can be seen as this: Lester needs to challenge all of his previously held ideas about life, and Carolyn is still contained by the status quo. He needs to change and is trying to, and she is unwilling and unable. *American Beauty* is about the dysfunction that arises when husbands and wives refuse to address marital problems and change.

When we understand that our protagonists and antagonists are people who are shaped by their values and beliefs, we see that they stand for these ideas in drama. When their conflict is constructed in clearly understood oppositions, the ideas behind the story become stronger and more powerful, because they are dramatized in action. In thrillers, as well as horror and most action movies, villains define the main problem for protagonists. But in drama, comedy, and other genres, antagonists don't always form the main conflict for the protagonist; they're often only part of it. Take *Jerry Maguire*. The main conflict for Jerry isn't if he can he beat Bob Sugar (Jay Mohr), his competition at the agency. The real conflict for Jerry is, can he be a successful sports agent and lead a meaningful life? Jerry conflicts with Bob Sugar, Dorothy

(Renée Zellweger), Rod Tidwell (Cuba Gooding Jr.), and his clients. Certainly, Bob Sugar is used as an antagonist for parts of the movie, but he is more there for contrast. Jerry is caught in a crisis of conscience, and Bob probably wasn't born with one.

In *American Beauty*, Carolyn is Lester's antagonist. But there are other difficulties he encounters, with his job and his daughter. Even in *Jaws*, in which the conflict is with the shark (a force of nature that is really played as the antagonist), Chief Brody is opposed for the first part of the movie by the town, represented by the mayor. The chief wants to close the beaches, and the mayor won't let him.

MEANINGFUL CONFLICT

To fully appreciate a story, however, it's not enough just to understand the conflict as strong oppositions. The audience must grasp the nature of the conflict—where it comes from and what it means to the characters—for it to be truly effective. Whether we get the sources of conflict right at the start of a movie or are forced to wait as its causes are revealed through the drama, the audience is instinctively trying to make sense out of the problems the characters encounter. If we can't, the film starts to feel pointless, and our interest wanes.

If conflict is left only as a problem that has to be solved, unless the action is nonstop and entertaining as in the best James Bond films, the story becomes flat because there's been no effect on, and no consequence of the action and conflict for, the characters. Because the audience doesn't see how the conflict affects the protagonist and other main characters, they don't really know what it means to the characters. If the audience can't find this meaning, the story stays on the superficial level of plot action and has less of a chance of connecting with them. It's the difference between *Se7en* and *Panic Room*, both well-plotted thrillers, directed by the same director, David Fincher, but one rises to the level of American tragedy while the other congeals in melodrama that leaves you wondering what it was all for at the end.

Meaningful conflict expresses, through how the protagonist and other main characters cope and fare with the difficulties they encounter, basic human qualities, both positive and negative, that help us to understand the story, our world, and ourselves. Plots that incorporate scenes showing this response to conflict build stronger characters and stories (more on this later).

UNITY OF OPPOSITES: LOCKING THE CONFLICT

Once we have a clear concept of the conflict for the characters, we strengthen it by creating the connection that unites the two opposing forces in their struggle. We call this relationship *unity of opposites*. Unity of opposites is the unbreakable bond that exists between protagonist and antagonist (and sometimes even with other characters). It stands for whatever binds the opposing characters together and compels them to interact and clash. They cannot compromise. Only an underlying change in the dramatic situation or in one of the characters can stop the conflict, and this shift generally comes at the climax. These two characters in the personas of the protagonist and antagonist can be used several ways. They can be similar characters locked on opposing sides of a conflict, as in *Mr. & Mrs. Smith*. But more often they are two characters with diametrically opposed traits and qualities stuck together in the situation by a common problem or a common goal—e.g., Lester and Carolyn in *American Beauty* have the problem of their deteriorating marriage; Indiana Jones (Harrison Ford) and Rene Belloq (Paul Freeman) in *Raiders of the Lost Arc* are both after the Ark of the Covenant, which only one can possess.

Often the conflict can only end in the "death" of one of the characters. Death in drama doesn't necessarily mean human death. It can mean the destruction of a dominant trait or quality in one of the main characters. Look at *I ♥ Huckabees*. Brad (Jude Law) is the quintessentially upwardly mobile young man. Locked in his conflict with Albert (Jason Schwartzman) over the Open Coalition movement, he finally is forced to confront the conceits and pretense of his life and change. Or it can be actual death, as what Oliver (Michael Douglas) and Barbara (Kathleen Turner) Rose accomplish in *War of the Roses*. Family relationships keep conflicting characters in constant association (*American Beauty, About Schmidt*). Love can bring opposites together (*Annie Hall, The Break-Up*).

When the unity of opposites is clear and specific—the treasure map in *National Treasure*, the condo in *The Break-Up*, the father/daughter bond in *About Schmidt*—it strengthens a plot by providing specific reasons why characters in conflict must interact with each other until something significant has changed in the situation holding them together. In great films, the unity of opposites is unambiguous, clarifying what fuels the conflict and what characters must surrender for a resolution to be found.

THE THIRD FORCE: THE AGENT FOR CHANGE

Many new writers let the main conflict define their entire script—whether it's a problem with an antagonist or some major difficulty, natural or manmade. Again, unless the action is nonstop death defying or hysterically funny, it tends to be too narrow to hold our attention, and the drama becomes repetitive.

When we look at great films, we see they rarely rely on a single conflict to move their plots. There's the main problem, generally with the antagonist or main obstacle, and this has a line of action. But building alongside this is at least one other important line of action with a conflicting character or other difficulties for the protagonist. Sometimes this line builds to increasing conflict and creates more complications the deeper we go into the story. But often when it involves another character, after initial conflict, it resolves around the midpoint of the plot and develops positively for the protagonist, just as the real opposition for the story heats up. In the first half of the film, this plot line may support the main conflict or seem arbitrary when related to the main plot action. But by the second half, it affects the main plot line and merges with it.

When writers use this subplot, it does three important things. In the first half of a film, it adds tension to the beginning where the identity of the antagonist might only be hinted at and exposition is setting up the story. This makes the important information more interesting and creates worry for the audience about the welfare of the protagonist and other main characters.

Writers also use this subplot to develop the protagonist, getting her ready to face the antagonist. Based in a character who challenges the hero, this line of action alludes to other difficulties, internal or external, that she may need to overcome, before she is able to meet the antagonist (or main conflict) effectively.

Often this subplot character might seem like the antagonist but can be viewed more accurately as an *agent for change*. When used this way, the agent for change enters the story often as a new element in the protagonist's life (Mills in *Se7en*) or as someone returning from the protagonist's past (Ilsa [Ingrid Bergman] in *Casablanca*). He introduces new issues and causes new things to happen (George Baines [Harvey Keitel] in *The Piano*). She has goals and struggles to achieve them and conflicts with the protagonist until something gives and is transformed in their relationship (Rachel Lapp [Kelly McGillis] in *Witness*). Most times it's the protagonist who's learned something important and has grown from this interaction, leaving him able to meet the opposition and resolve the conflict at the main climax of the plot. This adversarial relationship forces the protagonist to confront himself in some way and change. Often the relationship is the basis for the protagonist's character arc, which charts his progress from one state to another.

Thirdly, when this subplot is effective, the protagonist creates a meaningful relationship with another character. This allows us to care more about the protagonist because we care about the relationship, and it leads to us becoming more involved in the film. Once the agent for change transforms into the protagonist's ally, the line of action affects the main plot line when the same forces opposing the protagonist threaten this character and their relationship. This raises the stakes for the hero and creates more tension in the second half.

In *Se7en*, the main conflict is about catching the serial killer. But the other important conflict describes the adversarial relationship between Somerset and Mills. Somerset starts the film intending to retire at the end of the week and withdraw from the world. Because of his relationship with Mills on this case, he decides to recommit and remain part of society. The relationship with Mills creates this arc.

This conflict is especially necessary to build tension as the exposition for the story is laid out in act one and the beginning of act two. Otherwise we'd have a potentially dull police procedural, where two men tackle a problem congenially, and less pressure builds. In the second act, the two men put their differences aside to work together, but there are still differences. By the middle of the movie, Mills is affecting Somerset, softening him. The older man starts mentoring his younger partner. This is when John Doe now physically enters the film and attacks, personally confronting

Mills when a lead takes them to Doe's apartment. Somerset's inner conflict finally resolves near the end of act two when he commits to staying on the case and working with Mills until the bitter end.

In *Casablanca*, many people think Ilsa is Rick's (Humphrey Bogart) antagonist. After all, she's Rick's main problem. But it's the Nazis who are our real villains, holding everyone hostage to papers and bureaucratic squabbling. Once Ilsa returns to Rick at the end of act two, he can finally act, and his action is to save Ilsa and foil the Nazis. She is responsible for his change, through her interaction with him.

Just to mix it up a little more, let's also say that sometimes the agent for change is the protagonist, who changes other characters around him. Look at Michael Mann's *Last of the Mohicans*. Hawkeye (Daniel Day Lewis) isn't changed by the action except in the sense that at the beginning he's without a mate and at the end he has one. But look at Cora's character (Madeline Stowe). She changes fundamentally, at first rejecting what Hawkeye stands for and then embracing it. Hawkeye even forces change upon Duncan (Steve Waddington), one of the antagonists in the film and Cora's British suitor. We find a similar dynamic in *The Fugitive*. Kimble (Harrison Ford) doesn't change, but Agent Gerard (Tommy Lee Jones) does by the end of the film—all owing to his interaction with the good doctor intent on finding his wife's killer.

The agent for change can also be the antagonist, too. In *Risky Business*, Lana (Rebecca De Mornay) functions for most of the movie as Joel's (Tom Cruise) antagonist. She creates the problems for him, forcing him to leave the safety of his middle-class suburban environment and ultimately to change. Even though Guido (Joe Pantoliano) orchestrates the climactic problem, it was only with Lana's helping hands. Or you can have a film like *Stranger than Fiction*, in which both protagonist Harold Crick (Will Ferrell) and antagonist Karen Eiffel (Emma Thompson) are changed by their encounter.

Besides adding tension and helping prepare your protagonist for the climax, the third force can also keep a plot from bogging down and becoming predictable. Because the agent for change introduces a new line of conflict affecting the protagonist, it makes it harder for the audience to guess the ultimate direction of the plot.

EMOTIONAL AND PHYSICAL CONFLICT

Another thing to remember about conflict is that it doesn't have to be physical and violent to be effective. Conflict can be subtle—emotional, sexual, intellectual. Audiences often relate far more quickly to emotional conflicts than ones involving guns, fist fights, car chases, and explosions. The reason for this is that we've all experienced emotional friction in our own lives, whereas not many of us have thrown a punch, or taken one for that matter. Look at such films as *Capote*, *Rain Man*, *The Hours*, *Erin Brockovich*, *Jerry Maguire*, and *Pride and Prejudice*. These films don't rely on bloodshed and carnage and still are satisfying and successful movies.

This doesn't mean films shouldn't use violence to make their points or to be true to their genres. Physical violence represents the meeting of uncompromising positions and so makes for good drama. Some films need violence to tell stories, just as dreams often use it to grab the dreamer's attention and illustrate their messages. In *Munich*, *Lord of the Rings*, *Se7en*, *Monster*, *Gladiator*, *North by Northwest*, *Million Dollar Baby*, and *City of God* violence moves the action. In many great films, physical violence is an intricate part of the story and contributes to its success. In *The Piano*, the emotional conflict between all of the characters escalates until it finally erupts with such brutality that it leaves the characters and audience stunned.

IMPORTANT CONFLICT VS. BIG CONFLICT

Many new writers worry that the conflict of their stories isn't "big enough" to be important to the audience. This often results in the pumping up of the main problem to melodramatic proportions. It becomes a "life or death" struggle, even if the problems don't really warrant it. These novice writers believe this is the only way to make the audience care about what happens. But because the action is conceived and played overdramatically, it usually rings false and undercuts the story. It may be do or die for the characters, but the audience really couldn't care less.

How do we get the audience to understand and care about what happens? It starts with making sure the problems and difficulties the protagonist faces are strong enough to drive a film ninety minutes to two hours long. Conflict strong enough to drive a feature depends on several things. Genre affects the conflict. A boy-meets-girl plot strategy isn't going to hold our attention in a horror film unless it's coupled with chills and thrills. But that same plot design has worked fine for countless comedies and romances. You have to understand your audience's expectations for excitement and appeal based on the genre within which you're writing. Then, whatever the genre, the problems have to challenge the hero in a serious way. This means the opposition presents a genuine danger to the protagonist's well-being—physical, emotional, or mental. In a thriller it may be the protagonist's life or the lives of his loved ones. In comedy, the protagonist's happiness or heart may be at stake.

With authentic jeopardy, the protagonist has something at risk. There have to be negatives, things he clearly does not want, awaiting him if he fails. The conflict affects him personally, and he cares about what happens. This means we *see* the effect of conflict on him, the positives and the negatives. When we see the effect, we better understand its importance to the hero—what's at stake for him if he fails—and it becomes important to us. (More on this later.)

The conflict must be seen not just as obstacles but also as life-changing events for your protagonist. What will your protagonist's encounter with conflict do to him? Not only will your character's circumstances be affected by this clash, but something fundamental in his being will be altered, too. These are the real stakes of your story, and the essence of drama.

Think of movies you care about. Are they all action oriented? Look at *American Beauty*, *Capote*, *Sideways*, *Tootsie*, *Rain Man*, *The Shawshank Redemption*, *Good Will Hunting*, *Field of Dreams*, *Moonstruck*. All of these films stress personal conflicts for the characters that are important and life changing for them. In most, the characters aren't threatened with physical death, but they do face the death of dreams, hopes, and aspirations. How they face these problems tells us about who they are and what the story means.

CONFLICT DEVELOPS POSITIVELY *AND* NEGATIVELY

As we plot out a story, we conceive it with the protagonist moving toward a goal and meeting with obstacles and complications along the way. Many writers give their heroes plenty of difficulties but don't use them effectively. The hero confronts the problem, solves it, and is on to the next one. The obstacles are simply hurdles for their protagonists to clear, and clear them they do.

But if each time your hero meets an obstacle, he overcomes it, how will your audience view him? They'll think he's capable, resourceful, and can handle anything. What kind of tension and doubt about his eventual success or failure will develop? Not very much, because we have to assume everything will work out fine. And suddenly, if it didn't, we might feel cheated and unsatisfied because the action goes counter to what we've seen built up in the plot.

In great films, the conflict develops both positively and negatively. We see the protagonist's successes and setbacks, and this creates the real tension that sustains a plot its entire length. We don't want the audience assuming everything is going to work out swell (and in most Hollywood movies we expect the endings to). We need to cast doubt on the hero's ultimate success, and we can only do this if the protagonist suffers real defeats along the way. But if he only experiences defeat, and then succeeds at the climax, this, too, will ring false. So he needs to fail as well as succeed as he works his way through the obstacles. We want the audience hoping for the best possible outcome, while fearing the worst will actually happen. When you achieve this, you've hooked the audience—reader or viewer.

As we study great films, we can identify scenes with positive, negative, and neutral outcomes. This is a great exercise anyone can do with her favorite movies. Keep a log of each scene, and as it ends, identify whether it has a positive, negative, or neutral effect on the characters and action. When you've finished the film, tally up each effect, and you'll find the negatives outweigh the positives every time. This is how tension escalates.

Let's look at just the opening of *Erin Brockovich*. The film begins with Erin in a job interview, and she's explaining why she desperately needs the position but is killing her prospects as she does. The following scene shows her leave the office and pause on the street, full of frustration. Next she reaches her car and discovers a parking ticket. It's just not her day. She gets in her car, drives up to a red light, and stops. The light turns green, she starts through the intersection, and BAM!—she gets hit. All of these first scenes are negatives. The next scene shows her with Ed Masery, and he assures her they'll make the man who hit her pay. Finally, we get a positive note. The next scene in court starts out well, but it soon goes awry when the defense counsel goes after Erin, whose verbal explosion causes her to lose the case—a real negative. In the hall, she blows up at Ed and blames him for telling her she'd win.

The progression of these scenes shows the development of the conflict, illustrates who Erin is at the start of the film, and sets up her relationship with Ed Masery, the man who will eventually hire her and allow her to succeed. But the sequence also set the odds overwhelmingly against her.

In a plot, successes gain your protagonist something along the way, but often they are only temporary solutions. At the end of the first act of *Tootsie*, Michael (Dustin Hoffman) gets the part in the soap opera. He'll have the money to mount roommate Jeff's (Bill Murray) play (his goal). He's solved his problem. Except when he actually begins work, then all the other problems start. In *Risky Business*, Joel thinks he's solved his problem with Lana over his mother's Steuben Egg numerous times only to be proved wrong. In *Wedding Crashers*, John (Owen Wilson) seems to be getting closer to Claire (Rachel McAdams) at several occasions in the plot only to lose her.

THE IMPORTANCE OF FAILURE TO YOUR PROTAGONIST'S CHARACTER ARC

This leads us to the importance of failure. Obviously, failure helps create suspense, especially if we're on the protagonist's side and care about him. We keep hoping he'll get on his feet and make progress toward his goal in the face of these defeats. But how will he? Through his failure, if he can confront it.

Failure is a terrific teacher for a worthy protagonist. What does your audience know about people? We know we don't change easily. We only change as a result of things not working—failure. If everything goes great, is there any reason for you to change? Obviously not. But when conflict throws its monkey wrench into your plans, and you come up against problems that are larger than you, you have to grow to be able to meet them, or you don't get what you want. This is true in life and it's true in drama. Something dramatic has to happen for people to realize they must alter their style, beliefs, or ideas. Your characters need conflict to force change upon them.

If characters don't change in the face of failure, they don't succeed, and your story falters (unless, of course, this is your point). Or if they succeed with no change, the victory seems hollow and unearned. The heart of great drama is change. The impact of a truly powerful conflict on a protagonist creates the transforming action that brings about something new and different. Understand that your audience is interested in seeing characters face problems and learn to deal with them.

Failure is the key to your protagonist's character arc. How he responds to a crisis will develop the depth of his personality and your audience's relationship with him. This is especially true of setbacks. Is he disillusioned and defeated? Or is he galvanized and determined? A plot deepens and grows by including scenes that show the protagonist's reactions to the ordeals he goes through and the effects the conflict has on him.

Conflict is key to plotting a great story. It defines the parameters of the story, helps to generate tension and suspense, and shapes your audience's experience of the characters. When conflict is properly conceived and handled, the story has the best chance of fulfilling the audience's expectations, not because they're able to predict what's going to happen and how the story will end, but because they've been in doubt about it throughout the film.

CHAPTER 4

THE PRINCIPLES OF ACTION

Once conflict is conceived, it has to be set in motion. In the language of drama, this means characters must be motivated to achieve their goals. We don't want to sit around with someone waiting for something to happen. We want to see characters *make* things happen. We want to watch them *act*.

In the best films, the action of the plot is based on who the characters are, what they want and need, and what their motivations are. The characters' goals, specifically the protagonist's, draw them to push the action forward and struggle with the obstacles along the way. They meet with conflict that develops positively and negatively, one episode into another, until they reach the final climax and resolution. A good plot relies on the action of the story moving forward to create basic momentum, but it must also include scenes that reveal why this story is happening, what's at stake for the protagonist and other characters, what the conflict means to them (and us), and the consequences of their actions and choices along the way. All of this has to be orchestrated for the audience into an understandable and meaningful whole.

It's often said that good plot evolves naturally from the reaction of a character in a dramatic situation. But this is not enough. When we make drama, it's not the same as listening to grandma tell us a bedtime story. The audience is seeing a story unfold. Some of the information is explicit, and some of it is implicit in the subtext. The audience has work to do to stay involved; they must put pieces of the story's information together. And when they do this, then they become active participants in the creation of the work, and they're involved in the story. If everything is spoon-fed to them, and there's nothing to figure out, they become bored because of the passive nature of viewing.

As you orchestrate the action of your characters, you're really leading your audience through your story. As the storyteller, you're the guide, the Gurkha. We guide our audience through the material, its peaks and valleys, by creating a plot with strong relationships between the scenes. This is the real language of drama—understanding how these relationships work and how best to exploit them for the purpose of your story.

All great plots, linear and nonlinear, are based on the laws of causality. One action causes another action, and this causes another, and so on. The audience sees these relationships between the scenes and so can draw conclusions or infer information to create meaning and follow along.

The principles of action describe three sets of scene relationships that help us weave all the plot threads of a story together. This is what creates real narrative momentum. If there is little or no relationship between the scenes, meaning is lost and audience interest sags. Screenwriters build these strong causal relationships through the following:

- Cause-and-effect scene relationships
- Rising conflict
- Foreshadowing conflict

CAUSE-AND-EFFECT SCENE RELATIONSHIPS

All plotting is based in cause-and-effect scene relationships. This is the simplest but strongest plotting tool and yet the least understood and most ill used.

In the first chapter, we talked about causality as being instrumental in pushing the story action forward, ensuring the audience understands what's going on, and creating forward momentum. A strong plot is *not* a timeline of events that occur in sequence. Scenes have to be connected to each other for the audience to understand the film's true meaning. A plot is developed through characters' actions that lead to reactions and consequences that in turn create more reactions and consequences the characters must face. The language of drama depends on this: We need to see the cause and the effect, the *action and reaction*, to follow along and understand what's going on and why.

Consider three scenes from a screenplay a writer was working on with me: 1) A guy and a girl fight and break up. 2) The guy sits in a café, drinking a latte and reading a report for work. 3) The guy is at home getting ready to go out. How are you supposed to understand these scenes? There seems to be no connection between them. We don't know how the guy felt about his girlfriend. Nor do we know what he's getting ready for. My student wrote these scenes thinking she was *showing* her character. Instead, she slowed her story's momentum, revealed nothing important about the character, and did little to expose the meaning of the conflict in the first scene. She explained in a consultation that in scene two the guy is really upset about his fight in scene one, but the action of the scene shows none of it. In scene three, he's on his way to apologize. From what was on the page, there is no way a reader or viewer would know how the guy felt about what happened, so she will assume he feels nothing. If scripts are made up of seemingly non-related events (where scene relationships are not clear), the reader loses interest because there seems to be no point.

Now if slight alterations were made to link the scenes, they would draw the reader through them and build to a point. Consider these scenes again, with changes in italics. 1) A guy and a girl fight and break up. 2) The guy sits in a café, drinking a latte and *looking at* a report for work, *but he can't concentrate. An old card falls out of the papers. On it are the words "I'll always love you." He contemplates it. After a moment, he picks up his stuff and leaves.* 3) The guy is at home getting ready to go out. *He looks at a photograph of the girl on his bureau and picks up a bouquet of flowers.*

In this sequence, we can see how one scene leads to another. We understand that the fight affected him, and he's going to his girl to make up. Whether he gets to her or not doesn't matter; the scenes are understandable and have purpose because they show action and reaction instead of inaction.

There is an old rule of screenwriting that says, "Show. Don't tell." It's a great rule, but it often leads a new writer to think that if she shows her character doing something—e.g., studying, then going to the museum, and then reading the *New York Times*—she's revealing who the character is, in this case an intellectual. The problem is that these scenes will be quickly forgotten. They may reveal some aspect of the character's life, but they're not engaging us or building story momentum. If too many of these scenes come in the middle or late in the story, they slow the plot's momentum. The protagonist comes across as passive because the action feels unmotivated and not directed. The rule ought to be revised to read, "Dramatize! Don't tell."

Plot *dramatizes* the hero's pursuit of his overall story goal, along with his interim goals, through his encounter with conflict—obstacles and complications—and then shows the consequences that result from his actions. The audience follows along, understanding what's happening and assigning meaning to the events. These cause-and-effect scene relationships break into two types: simple and complex. Simple cause-and-effect scene relationships relate to logical action; complex relationships give us deeper characterizations.

Simple Cause-and-Effect Scene Relationships

Simple cause-and-effect scene relationships show the connections between actions and events and guide the audience through the information of the story so that they understand and remember exactly what's going on. The clearest examples of these types of scene relationships are seen in investigative pieces like detective stories, police procedurals, and legal dramas, in which the protagonist has a specific goal. But every genre relies on these scene relationships.

In the last chapter we used the opening of *Erin Brockovich* to examine how conflict develops positively and negatively. But let's look at those scenes again to see how they're linked.

The first scenes set up Erin's difficulty in finding a job and her accident. The audience sees her drive up to the red light, wait for it to turn green, go, and then get hit. These scenes are all connected because of the job interview. In real life, who knows how Erin Brockovich had her accident. But in the movie, the scenes build a sequence of events in cause-and-effect plotting. The next scene doesn't show Erin in an ambulance or at the ER. Instead it's months later, and Erin, in a neck brace, meets Ed Masery, a lawyer who assures her that the guilty party will pay.

Next we see Erin in court (the filmmakers don't spend time

developing the case, jumping over all of it). Ed's questioning of Erin on the stand starts well, but the cross-examination by the defense counsel kills her, and she loses her temper and the case. Angry and blaming Ed, she storms off. The next scene introduces her children and that her babysitter is moving away. Erin has nothing to feed them, and despite having little money, she takes them out to dinner, letting them believe she's won the case and everything will be fine. Then she's back looking for a job, where she started at the beginning. But the point of this sequence is that Erin has met Ed. When she is unable to find employment, not knowing what else to do, she returns to Ed's law offices and begs him for a job. He relents and hires her, fourteen minutes into the film.

The purpose of these first scenes is that Erin is now working in Ed's office. This puts her on track to discover the paperwork on the PG&E case in the files of Donna Jensen's real estate negotiation, which is the substance of the film. That's the story. These scenes plot out, through cause-and-effect scene relationships, a progression that leads through conflict to this result. We don't simply see the character doing one thing, then another, and then something else. A logical progression of plot action develops and creates meaning we understand. Many new writers write scenes that show the protagonist dealing with different aspects of his life, feeling that this is how to reveal character. You can get away with this early in a movie, when you're setting things up, but the deeper in you go, plotting action and conflict has to take hold, connecting scenes to each other to sustain the audience's interest.

In *Chinatown*, the first part of the plot dramatizes Gittes (Jack Nicholson) following Mulray (Darrell Zwerling), trying to discover if the water commissioner is having an affair. By way of Gittes's surveillance, the filmmakers plant information that the audience is going to need later in the film to grasp what happens. Each scene gives exposition about the drought, the farmers in the valley, the dried riverbed, and the water run-off at the ocean. The action shows Gittes shadowing his man, trying to ascertain what is true, while the audience learns with him what's going on.

About fourteen minutes into the movie, Gittes has followed Mulray to the coast. It's evening. While watching from the cliffs, he hears a rumbling. Not knowing what it is, he moves onto a culvert overlooking the ocean and promptly gets soaked by the run-off of water. Mad, he returns to his car parked at Point Fermin Park and finds a handbill on his windshield referring to city hall and the drought. He grabs a cheap pocket watch from a pile in his glove compartment, places it underneath the tire of Mulray's tire, and leaves. The next scene, back at Gittes's office, starts on a broken pocket watch telling us how late Mulray was at the beach. These scenes lead one to the next, ensuring that the audience will be able to make sense of what's going on.

If scenes have little or no effect on those immediately following them, your audience has to search for connections to understand why you're showing them what you are. This slows the film's pacing. And there's no guarantee the audience will understand the scenes the way you've intended them. Also, if the reactive influence of the scenes isn't made clear until many scenes later, momentum will break down and your protagonist will appear passive, resulting in your audience losing patience with him and your story.

Complex Cause-and-Effect Scene Relationships

In complex cause-and-effect scene relationships, we're interested in revealing the characters. Our focus is on how the action and conflict, desire and resistance, intersect and affect these characters. A successful plot doesn't focus solely on the scenes that show the active pursuit of the goal or the points of active conflict with the antagonist and other obstacles; it includes the *reactions* of the main characters, especially the protagonist, to the obstacles, complications, setbacks, and successes he encounters along the way. It is the cause and the effect, the action and reaction, that create meaning and drive a plot forward. Because the hero's overall story goal isn't resolved until the end of the film, we're dramatizing his steps as he pursues his goal and *what happens as a result of his actions*.

Now what happens when you show the characters' reactions to the conflict? You reveal who the character really is. Remember that old adage your mother used to admonish you with: Actions speak louder than words. It's not what characters tell us about themselves, or even the things you show us about them in their everyday lives that matters. What counts is how your character behaves when the chips are down and the pressure is on. That's when you reveal the true person behind the mask. And that's what the audience is waiting for.

Again, from *Erin Brockovich*, we find Erin working on the case. Around the midpoint of the film, another couple has come forward to talk to her about their medical problems. Erin goes back to Hinkley to find others who might be affected. She meets Rita and Ted Daniel (Cordelia Richards and Wade Williams) whose daughter Annabelle (Kristina Malota) has cancer. Her head wrapped, presumably because of the effects of chemotherapy, Annabelle snuggles in a nightgown between her parents while Erin talks to them. But instead of discussing the lawsuit, Erin focuses on Annabelle and keeps the conversation light, complimenting the girl and smiling at her, although in Erin's eyes we see how affected she is. The director emphasizes Erin's connection with the girl. But the next scene shows Erin driving home, eyes staring straight ahead, intense and clearly disturbed by what she's experienced. The following scene shows her with Ed the next day, trying to talk him into expanding the Jensen's case into a class-action suit against PG&E. Ed will have none of it. But Erin is nothing if not tenacious. She dogs him obstinately into the office, where he finally relents and gives her the OK to talk to other people.

What does this sequence show about Erin that is so important? That she's affected by the plight of these people and she wants to do something. It allows the audience to understand her motivation for the next scene. By showing the character's reaction to the conflict, the audience better understands and knows her. It also allows viewers to share this emotional response with her, to have the time to process for themselves what she's endured. This is a stronger means to reveal character than by just including scenes of Erin describing how much she cares about other people. In earlier drafts of the script, Academy Award–winning writer Susannah Grant included a scene of Erin at home, unable to sleep, checking her own children and verbalizing to George all these feelings. Instead, the film uses a visual emotional reaction that communicates completely what we need to feel to understand the next scene.

Effective plotting incorporates action and reaction, cause and effect, to build momentum and deepen the audience's involvement in the story. We use action to propel the forward motion of the story; reaction to show the consequences the actions have on the characters and allow the audience to feel with them. When we show what characters experience as a result of their actions, and how that motivates new actions, the audience understands and empathizes with the characters better. Remember: *Plot is more than an outline of events; it's the ordering of emotions.* When we dramatize the emotional side of a story, we add dimension. Complex cause-and-effect scene relationships emphasize the action and its effect on the character.

Strong films build with one action causing a reaction, and this produces another, and so on. Whether these scene relationships are simple or complex, they create a sense of mounting action.

They keep your protagonist on track and not wandering from scene to scene, making your transitions stronger because one action leads to another.

RISING CONFLICT

Rising conflict intensifies the causal relationships between the scenes. Based in cause-and-effect plotting, it's focused on escalating the struggle. It orchestrates the actions between the protagonist and antagonist or the protagonist and major obstacles and results in building more tension. When rising action is used in the protagonist/antagonist axis, it spotlights the conflict stemming from the wants and needs of these oppositional characters. One makes a move and the other counters. This provokes a more concentrated response, an attack, which leads to subsequent counterattacks.

There is a sequence in *Casablanca* that starts with Victor Laszlo (Paul Henreid) trying to talk Rick (Humphrey Bogart) into giving him the Letters of Transit. Downstairs, the Germans start singing "Wacht am Rhein." Laszlo reacts and heads into the bar, where he counters this assault to his cause by firing up the orchestra to play the French national anthem. After a nod from Rick, the orchestra starts, and Laszlo leads the other French nationals in a rousing rendition of the "Marseillaise." The crowd jumps to their feet, competing with the Germans, and finally drowning them out. The Germans sink into their chairs, defeated, while Laszlo finishes. Then, Major Strasser (Conrad Veidt) counters by ordering Renault (Claude Raines) to close Rick's saloon. The sequence continues with Strasser then coming to Ilsa and threatening Laszlo's life.

This is a very sharp example of rising conflict. It is move and countermove, attack and counterattack, driving up the stakes of the story for the characters, contained basically in two scenes, beat by beat. But scenes building a rising conflict don't have to come on the heels of each other, with one character immediately responding to the other. Instead, we often see the conflict as it plays out over a larger sequence of scenes. These are crisis scenes for the protagonist in which you show him dealing with a threat, obstacle, or problem. Then you show the effect of this action before moving to other characters and their responses.

At the midpoint of *Jaws*, the shark narrowly misses Chief Brody's son in the pond and a boater gets killed. Brody forces the mayor to hire Quint (Robert Shaw) to hunt the shark. This is their response to the shark's attacks, their countermove. Brody, Hooper, and Quint sail off. They bait and wait. The shark arrives, takes the bait, and breaks the line. They go back to "chumming," throwing the bait overboard, and waiting. Finally, the shark surfaces ("I think we're going to need a bigger boat") and the battle is on. They harpoon the shark, sinking three lines into the beast, but still it gets away. That evening, while comparing "war stories," Quint reveals his back story on the USS *Indianapolis*, and we get more exposition and a great tale. As he ends, the shark attacks the boat again, this time disabling it. The next morning finds the men trying to fix the boat and head in, but instead they're taking on water.

To increase tension, the orchestration of scenes that build rising conflict comes more frequently in the second half of a screenplay or movie. Here the attacks and counterattacks increase and become more serious and threatening to the hero. As these confrontations escalate, they lead directly to the last crisis and main climax. If the protagonist and antagonist are locked together with strong unity, and evenly matched with the antagonist a little stronger, real tension results.

If your story doesn't have a specific antagonist to pit against your protagonist, the obstacles standing between him and his goal must intensify and become more threatening to his success in the second half of the film. In movies like *Jerry Maguire* and *American Beauty*, conflict redoubles, even as it doesn't come from one specific source. In *Jerry Maguire*, from the midpoint on, Jerry only has one client. Although he and Dorothy start dating, Rod doesn't get his offer, and then Dorothy takes another job in San Diego. This prompts Jerry to ask her to marry him. But by the end of the wedding both know it was a mistake. In act three, Dorothy realizes Jerry's problems with commitment and intimacy and breaks away from him. And at Rod's big game, Bob Sugar turns up, trying to steal him from Jerry. Then Rod takes a hit on the field that knocks him out, and there's doubt he'll ever get up again. It looks as though Jerry might lose everything.

In *American Beauty*, Lester is the main protagonist and Carolyn his antagonist, but each of the secondary characters—Jane and Ricky—has desires and conflicts, too. These lines of action are orchestrated around Lester's through-line. Acts one and two show the rising conflict between Lester and Carolyn, along with developing Ricky's problems with his father, Col. Fitts (Chris Cooper), and Jane's growing disenchantment with Angela. Lester and Carolyn's marriage is in trouble from the start, and they're not relating. He starts not caring what she thinks; she retaliates by starting the affair with Buddy (Peter Gallagher). In act three, Lester is no longer in conflict with Carolyn. But Jane and Angela are fighting, Col. Fitts has kicked Ricky out of the house, and Buddy has broken up with Carolyn, sending her into a rage.

Below are plot breakdowns for *Jaws* and *American Beauty*, two movies in which rising conflict is clearly discernible. Several things are apparent from these breakdowns. You can see in the first column on the left what the scenes are presenting in the form of action: exposition, developments, plans, etc. (For further definition of these terms, see the next chapter.) The second column notes the time the event takes place in the movie. The third column gives a brief description of the action or event. The fourth column gives more notes, and the last shows whether the outcome was positive, negative, or neutral (denoted by an "o"). If you look at the second half of each diagram, you'll see crisis scenes mounting, orchestrating the rising conflict in attacks and counterattacks between the men and the shark in *Jaws* and all of the characters in *American Beauty*. You'll also notice that there are more failures and setbacks than successes for the protagonists.

Jaws–Plot Breakdown–Rising Conflict

Plot/Definition	Time	Action/Event	Notes	Out-come
ACT 1 Main Exposition	:00:26	Beach party fun	Happy college folks	+
The Problem	:03:00	Fun turns deadly Introduces Chief	First Attack Call to action	-
Main Exposition	:04:20	Brody (CB) and family; CB learns of problem		-/+
Development	:05:45	CB goes to investigate	Movement	o
Exposition	:06:35	Gets story from young man		o
Development	:07:05	Body discovered; shark attack		-
Exposition	:07:11	Shark attack	CB responds with action	+
New Plan	:08:40	"Beach closed" signs		+
Problem/Crisis	:10:00	CB learns of Boy Scouts boat test	Acts to head them off	-/+
Obstacle/ Reversal	:10:30	Mayor stops beach closing	"Boat accident"	-
Development	:12:38	People go to the beach	Suspense	o
Problem/ Attack	:16:15	Child killed; mother bereft	Attack	-
New Plan Exposition	:17:15	Reward offered at meeting; Quint's intro; exposition on shark	Response-action	o/+

Plot/Definition	Time	Action/Event	Notes	Out-come
Counter-Attack	:21:30	Beach closed; hunters head out	Rising conflict	o
Exposition	:21:38	CB researching in shark book	Tension mounting	-
Conflict	:22:10-:26:43	Intercut CB, hunters and shark	Rising conflict	o/+
Attack	:22:34	Drunk men on dock		-
Counter-Attack	:25:08	Shark takes bait and almost eats man		+
Result	:26:43	A narrow escape		-/+
Conflict/ Development	:27:00	CB trying to manage hunters	Matt Hooper (MH) arrives –shark expert	
Development	:30:00	At the morgue, MH says: "This is not a boat accident!"	Confirms CB's initial response	+
Climax	:31:46	Shark caught; MH says not the one	Problem appears solved	+/-
Development	:35:05	Mrs. Kitner slaps CB		-
Act 1 Climax	:36:50	CB accepts responsibility	CB feels guilty for failing	-
ACT 2 Response/ NewPlan	:36:56	CB feels bad; MH stirs to action		-/+
Action	:42:26	Cut open shark: no boy	CB must close the beach	o
Action/ Exposition	:44:18	Investigate feeding grounds	Anticipate shark attack	-
Discovery	:46:35-:49:00	Find Gardner's boat, body, and shark tooth	Lose evidence	-
Obstacle	:49:20	Close the beach; Mayor refuses		-
Development	:52:28	Beaches open; tourists arrive; Media; mayor; people	CB and MH patrolling	-
Rising Conflict	:55:55	People in; CB sends son to pond	Tension mounting	-
Crisis	:58:09	Shark fin spotted; can't shoot	Conflict	-
Reversal	:59:54	Kids!		-/+
Reversal	1:00:26	Shark in pond; man killed; CB's son traumatized	Attack	-

Plot/Definition	Time	Action/Event	Notes	Out-come
Midpoint	1:03:30	CB forces Mayor to hire Quint	Overcomes obstacle	+
Preparations	1:05:10	Quint prepares		+
Action	1:11:00	Out they go		o
Action/Move	1:11:40	Bait the shark; wait	Waiting	o
Counter-move	1:13:18	Shark takes bait; line breaks	Counter-attack	+/-
Plans/ Exposition	1:18:30	Deciding where to go, etc.		
Obstacle/ Attack	1:19:00	"We're going to need a bigger boat!"	Confrontation; gets away	-
Exposition	1:25:25	USS *Indianapolis*	Calm before the storm	+/-
Attack/Climax	1:33:05	Shark attacks; boat disabled	Helpless; complication	-
Act 2 Climax			Consequences	
ACT 3 Plans/Obstacle	1:35:20	Repair boat; shark attacks	Survive attack	+/-
Complication	1:37:30	Quint destroys radio	Quint going crazy	-
Attack	1:40:00	Shark chasing; pushing boat	Got them on the run	-
Retreat/Crisis	1:47:00	Heading in; engine breaks	Complication	-
Act 3 Climax begins				
Obstacle/Crisis	1:47:50	Boat sinking; life jackets come out	Facing the end	-
The New Plan	1:49:15	MH remembers underwater cage	New hope	+
Confrontation	1:51:45	MH goes under; shark destroys cage	Rising conflict; attacks and counter-attacks	-
Attacks and	1:56:40	Shark attacks, boat sinks; Quint dies	Rising conflict	-
Counter-Attacks	1:57:00	Boat sinking; CB gets off one good shot	Rising conflict	+
Act 3 Climax		Shark explodes	Success!	+
Resolution	1:59:00	MH surfaces; CB and MH swim in		+

American Beauty—Plot Breakdown—Rising Conflict

Plot/Definition	Time	Action/Event	Notes	Out-come
ACT 1 The Problem	:00:30	Jane on tape with Ricky	"I need a father who's a role model."	-
The Problem	:01:00	End of tape	"You want me to kill him?"	-
Main Exposition Foreshadowing	:01:15	Lester's voice over introduces story	"I'll be dead in a year... But it's never too late..."	-
Exposition	:02:15	Introduce Carolyn	"We used to be happy."	-
Exposition	:03:16	Introduce Jane	She thinks he's a loser	-
Exposition/ Conflict	:05:00	Lester's job in jeopardy	Want him to justify job	-
Exposition	:06:15	The new gay neighbors	A happy couple	o
Crisis/Attack	:07:05	At dinner, Lester tries to talk to Jane; can't confront wife	The unhappy family; no one gets along	-
Exposition	:09:12	Intro Ricky and his camera	Ricky watches Lester and Jane	-
Exposition/ Obstacle	:10:20	Carolyn's real estate job	Carolyn's self-loathing	-
New Plan	:13:56	Parents come to see Jane perform at basketball game	Carolyn's version of fostering "family" values	+/-
Inciting Incident	:15:56	Lester sees Angela	Fantasy engages	-
Result	:19:03	"I've awakened from a coma"	"Spectacular!"	+
Exposition	:20:00	Establish Angela's dream	Angela self-assured	
Development	:21:16	Ricky videotaping Jane	She likes it though says not	+
Decision/Action	:22:20	Lester sneaks Angela's number and calls her while Jane showers	Tension mounting	-
New Development	:22:34	Introduce Ricky's family	Meet Col. Fitts; establish homophobic attitude	-

Plot/Definition	Time	Action/Event	Notes	Out-come
Complication	:28:10	Jane meets Ricky at school	She doesn't know what to make of him	-
Development/ Conflict	:30:30	Carolyn's real estate banquet	Lester doesn't want to go	-
Development	:32:30	Lester meets Ricky		o
Complication	:33:00	Carolyn makes lunch date	Carolyn in awe of Buddy	+
Development	:33:45	Ricky gets Lester high	Ricky quits; Lester's new hero	+
Move	:35:45	Lester and Carolyn arrive home	Angela flirts with Lester	+/-
Complication	:37:47	Lester overhears Angela say she'd screw him	Lester's happy	+
Conflict	:37:30	Jane sees Ricky's fiery message	Jane learns he was institutionalized	o
<u>Act 1 Climax—The Plan</u>	:39:40	Lester starts working out	He's going for Angela	+/-
ACT 2 Attack	:41:15	Fitts wants Ricky's urine sample	Ricky's under lock and key	-
Complication	:42:30	Lester dreams of Angela		+
Attack/ Counterattack	:44:49	Carolyn catches him masturbating	Lester fights back and wins	+
Development	:47:45	Lester comes to Ricky for dope		
Conflict	:50:00	Carolyn discovers Lester and dope	Lester doesn't care	+
Obstacle/Crisis/ Attack	:51:20	Lester's job on the line; he quits and blackmails boss	Lester fights back and wins "Just an ordinary guy..."	+
New Plan	:53:00	Carolyn meets Buddy for lunch	Learn Buddy's wife left him	+/-
Development	:54:20	Ricky with Jane films dead bird	Ricky and Jane hit it off	+
Result/Attack	:55:25	Carolyn sleeps with Buddy	She attacks her marriage	-
<u>Midpoint—Decision</u>				
New Plan	:56:50	Lester at drive-thru; applies for job	Lester's trying to recapture youth; wants to change	+

Plot/Definition	Time	Action/Event	Notes	Out-come
Foreshadow Conflict	:57:40	Buddy takes Carolyn to the shooting range	Foreshadows murder stated at beginning	-
Development	:58:35	Jane and Ricky walking home	They're connecting	+
Foreshadow Conflict	1:00:00	Ricky shows Jane his father's Nazi paraphernalia and gun collection	Sets up another possible connection to death	-
Foreshadow Theme	1:02:00	Ricky shows Jane videotape of bag; they kiss		
Attack/ Counterattack	1:05:50	Carolyn makes Lester tell Jane about losing his job	Lester taking charge	+
Attack/ Counterattack	1:07:30	Carolyn tries to use Jane against Lester; Jane won't play		-
Consequence	1:09:00	Jane sees Ricky filming her	Jane shows herself to him	
Attack	1:10:00	Fitts attacks Ricky for showing Jane his stuff	Setting up more of Fitts's character	-
Foreshadowing	1:13:25	Carolyn enjoying shooting range		+
Complication	1:14:45	Carolyn sees Lester's Firebird		-
Desire/Obstacle	1:15:56	Lester tries to reach Carolyn	They almost connect; hit theme of materialism	+/-
Exposition	1:18:30	Jane turns camera on Ricky; he doesn't hate Dad	Jane doesn't mean her original threat	+
Foreshadowing Conflict	1:23:26	Lester's V.O. indicates this is the day he dies		-
Confrontation	1:24:22	Set up Angela staying over; Jane confronts Lester on actions	Lester attacks back	-
Development	1:25:20	Fitts watches Lester and Ricky	Fitts suspicious	-
Complication	1:26:00	Fitts finds video of Lester	Makes him suspicious	-

Plot/Definition	Time	Action/Event	Notes	Out-come
Act 2 Climax—Crisis	1:27:00	Carolyn drives through Mr. Smiley's with Buddy	Lester discovers her affair; Marriage over; he's free	+
ACT 3 Consequence	1:28:23	Buddy breaks up with Carolyn	Carolyn despondent	-
Complication	1:29:30	Lester working out; needs pot	Lester calls Ricky	o
Attack	1:30:30	Angela pushes Jane about Ricky	Jane doesn't want to tell her	-
Complication	1:31:10	Fitts sees Ricky sell Lester the pot	Fitts misconstrues meaning	-
Attack/ Counterattack	1:32:35	Angela comes on to Lester; he reciprocates	Angela intimidated; Lester baffled by her response	o
Attack/ Counterattack	1:33:25	Fitts busts Ricky over Lester	Ricky fights back	-
Result	1:34:15	Ricky says goodbye to Mom		-
New Plan	1:36:25	Carolyn listens to motivational tapes in car	"I refuse to be a victim"	+
Attack	1:37:00	Jane and Angela argue over Ricky and Lester; Ricky tells Angela off	Tension rising: "Please don't fuck my Dad."	-/+
Consequence	1:38:20	Angela cries on the stairs		
Complication	1:38:45	Fitts comes on to Lester	Lester gently rebuffs him	-
Foreshadowing Conflict	1:41:30	Carolyn reveals gun in car	She blames Lester	-
Discovery	1:42:20	Lester discovers Angela	The seduction begins	-
Foreshadowing Conflict	1:42:55	Carolyn on her way home	Will she discover Lester?	-
Rising Conflict	1:43:00	Lester wants Angela	They get closer	-/+
Exposition	1:43:40	Ricky and Jane plan to runaway	Parents' different attitudes	o
Crisis	1:45:45	Angela reveals it's her first time	Lester's humanity comes out	-
Crisis	1:48:40	Carolyn pulls up		

Plot/Definition	Time	Action/Event	Notes	Out-come
Result	1:48:18	Lester asks Angela about Jane	Learns she's in love; Lester happy	+
Act 3 Climax — Crisis Attack	1:51:35	Lester looking at photo of happier times, is killed	Theme hit	-/+
Resolution	1:52:00	Jane and Ricky discover body	Voiceover starts; theme	o/+
Reveal	1:54:12	Fitts with missing gun from case	Voiceover continues	+
Resolution of Theme	1:55:00	Ricky's videotape of bag	Voiceover of all the beauty in the world	+

In action films like *Jaws*, *Spider-Man*, and *Die Hard*, it's easy to see scenes building together in a rising conflict. Characters in specific scenes make moves and countermoves toward their objectives and attack and counterattack to achieve their goals. We see definite moves on each side as the characters try to control the situation and attain their ends. But plotting a rising conflict is a part of every great movie, where the difficulties the protagonist faces the later we get in the film have to increase in intensity and danger. Whether your film is *The Matrix*, *American Beauty*, or *Wedding Crashers*, the threats to the characters have to increase to keep your audience with you and interested. Look at *American Beauty* and you'll see conflict is ever-present. From just after the midpoint, when Lester quits his job until the end, we see rising conflict building with all the characters in their separate and joined story lines. In *Wedding Crashers*, Trap (David Conrad) goes after John (Owen Wilson) the moment he perceives Claire's (Rachel McAdams) interest in him, and the rising conflict just keeps building back and forth from there.

FORESHADOWING CONFLICT

In the second half of *Jaws*, the first day on the water ends with the men drinking down below on Quint's boat, the *Orca*, sharing "war stories." As the sun sets on them, the audience sees a lone yellow barrel crack the surface not far from the boat. It says the shark is close by.

To simply *foreshadow* means to indicate or suggest beforehand that something is going to happen. To foreshadow conflict means you're specifically making your audience anticipate difficulties ahead. You alert them that something unpleasant, maybe threatening, is near. They know it's coming, they can feel it, but they just don't know when it will appear, and so it builds tension.

Horror films foreshadow conflict all the time, but most films rely on this technique of plotting to build tension. Remember *Signs*? Just look at how much suspense and anxiety M. Night Shyamalan wrung out of the audience in the first half of his film. From the setup of the crop circles to the Hesses' dog barking uncontrollably at something hidden within the corn, excited uncertainty mounts in the audience as they anticipate trouble in the future of the characters.

Movies have music and sound effects to help build suspense and to presage ominous events. But in a script you have to create tension on the page. Here are some ideas to consider.

Uncompromising Characters

The starting point is to create strong, uncompromising characters locked in their situation, forced to interact and conflict with each other until the problem is worked out and resolved in some way. Look at the characters in *The Piano*. The protagonist, Ada (Holly Hunter), is willful, difficult, and unhappy; she refuses to speak and basically lives through her piano. Stewart (Sam Neil), the man her father has married her off to, is lonely and guarded. He wants a ready-made wife and family, so he takes Ada with her daughter, Flora (Anna Paquin), but the audience sees when he meets the family that he really has little empathy for Ada's condition. We know from the start of the movie, as Ada sets sail from Scotland for New Zealand, married to a man she's never met, that none of this bodes well. But the moment Stewart leaves the piano on the beach, we know this means war.

Or think of *Rain Man*. Charlie (Tom Cruise) is angry, impatient, and desperate for money as well as answers. Raymond (Dustin Hoffman) isn't capable of understanding his brother's predicament or helping; he needs care and patience. These two opposite characters are stuck together because of Charlie's half-baked plan to prove he can care for Raymond and thereby get his hands on his father's estate. We worry about Raymond's well-being and know Charlie's ideas will prove disastrous.

In *I ❤ Huckabees*, Albert is locked in a conflict with Brad Stand, and they couldn't be more opposite. Albert is a self-obsessed, insecure if well-intentioned neurotic. Brad is self-assured, successful, and smooth (at least at the start). Even though they're supposed to be on the same team, you know these two are bound to clash.

Show the Audience the Trouble Ahead

Another way to foreshadow conflict is to specifically show the audience the obstacles and problems that lie ahead of your hero. This can be especially strong when the audience knows about the obstacles before the protagonist does. Think of *The Lord of the Rings: The Two Towers*. The audience knows Gollum's own story about what happened to him since he found the ring. They know about Gollum's conflict over helping or betraying Frodo and fear for the hobbit, and they also see Frodo's condition worsen because of his possession of the ring. This heightens our concern for Frodo. Then, of course, there's the constant cutting to Mordor, showing the creation of the Uruk Hai army. What is the purpose of these scenes but to show the overwhelming odds against the small band of heroes?

Even direct foreshadowing works. In *American Beauty*, right from the beginning, Lester's voiceover tells us he's going to die. We know his death is in the future of the story, and this sets up tension that intensifies as we progress through the action. When it's hit again in narration, near the end of act two, the tension rises even more.

Good writers set up these fears so the audience will worry about the character's well-being. Sometimes foreshadowing can be an element fitted into a scene that is already focused on making other points in the plot. But the foreshadowing of conflict can also be the most important element at a certain juncture of the plot, and an entire scene is devoted to it.

Dangerous Props

Dangerous props are another way to hint at conflict to come. To paraphrase Russian playwright Anton Chekhov, If you introduce a gun, you must use the gun. Once something dangerous has been shown, the audience automatically remembers it and anticipates its use. In *American Beauty*, we've heard Jane ask Ricky to kill her father and Lester say he'll be dead in a year; we've seen Carolyn learn how to fire a gun with Buddy; we've gone to Ricky's house and seen his father's gun collection and Nazi memorabilia. How much more foreshadowing that something terrible is on the horizon does the audience need?

Other than dangerous props like guns, knives, and chain saws, showing disagreeable visuals will also raise the tension level. In *Se7en*, as Somerset investigates the opening murder scene, blood is shown splattered on a kitchen wall in the background. Then with each gruesome crime scene, the audience's anticipation of the horror grows.

Fearful Responses

Actions or circumstances that provoke fearful or painful responses from the characters also heighten tension. In *Casablanca*, Sam doesn't want to play the song for Ilsa, and his reactions tell us he's afraid to. Every time Mordor is mentioned in *The Lord of the Rings: The Two Towers* the stress level of the characters goes up, and so does the audience's. Every now and then narration is used to set a foreboding tone that sets up conflict to come. In *American Beauty*, Lester says he'll be dead within the year. In *The Good Girl*, Justine (Jennifer Aniston) discloses through her voiceover that she feels as though she's "on death row."

Foreshadowing is most often used in the first half of a film with cause-and-effect plotting while we're still setting up the second half when the rising conflict takes over. But it's a valuable tool that can come anywhere in a plot to help prepare the audience for conflict to come.

CHAPTER 5

THE TOOLS OF PLOTTING

In drama, action represents both form and content. The action and conflict aren't just the way you tell a story, but they convey the meaning of it, too. They shape a story's ideas through the characters' actions and reactions, and from these acts the audience grasps who the characters are. Great writers pay attention to the details of their characters' "doings" and behavior. They know that every act of a character, every decision and choice he makes, plays a part in how the audience perceives him, and they consider them carefully. They know that these actions let the audience know if the characters are worthy of their interest and empathy.

A successful plot depends on conflict and movement to build tension and momentum, while at the same time it must expose character and motivation to create meaning. The principles of action tell us scenes have to be related to one another for the audience to follow along. As we apply the principles of action, we find we have specific tools that help us with these functions. I call these action tools, character tools, and exposition tools.

ACTION TOOLS

These do just what they sound like: They create action that can be shown and dramatized. Your protagonist has a desire or need that drives him toward an objective. According to the first requirement of drama, this makes him active. The second requirement states he must meet with conflict. In plotting the scenes of a story, conflict appears in the form of obstacles and complications. If you've read books on screenwriting, or taken any classes, you should be well versed on these topics, but they're worth reviewing.

Obstacles

Obstacles are anything preventing the hero from reaching her goal. This goal can be a scene or intermediary goal or her overall goal of the movie. The best obstacles stir up the most conflict, incite the most action, and create a direct threat to the protagonist achieving her objective. When a protagonist meets an obstacle, if she is committed to her path, she must act and deal with it. She may confront it, flee it, or try to get around it, but she must do something about it.

Obstacles are pivotal to drama because they are crisis points in the plot. These are specific moments we can see in a story where conflict emerges and is dramatized. They add tension because as we watch the character (protagonist or other main character) grapple with the problems, we don't know how she will fare. Will the obstacle conquer the hero? Or will the hero overcome it? In theory, this doubt over the outcome creates more tension and suspense, drawing your audience deeper into the story as it plays out.

There are basically four types of obstacles:

- The antagonist
- Physical obstructions

- Internal conflicts
- Mystic forces or fate

In many films, the *antagonist* presents the principal conflict for the protagonist. An antagonist is a terrific device because he clearly characterizes the conflict and has a volitional will—the ability to consciously act against the protagonist. He actively works to defeat the hero, unlike a mere barrier—a bridge that's washed out or a car that won't start—that just stands in his way. The antagonist's will makes him a force to be reckoned with. But just because he's the antagonist doesn't mean he has to be villainous. Carolyn in *American Beauty* and Gus Portokalos (Michael Constantine) in *My Big Fat Greek Wedding* aren't bad or evil, but they both oppose the protagonists of their films in their overall goals.

Some films don't have a main antagonist as the central conflict but use one in different parts of the plot. In *The Best Years of Our Lives*, Al (Fredric March) is the obstacle blocking Fred (Dana Andrews) from getting together with Al's daughter Peggy (Teresa Wright), even though the men are friends. Remember, Bob Sugar in *Jerry Maguire* is used as an antagonist several times in the plot, but he doesn't constitute Jerry's real problem. He's just another obstacle Jerry has to face in his quest to fulfill his Mission Statement.

Physical obstructions are just what they sound like—any barrier that stands between your protagonist and her goal. These can be natural forces—the sea, desert, or jungle—or manmade, as in brick walls, car crashes, and dead ends. They are usually converted into specific elements. In *The Perfect Storm*, Capt. Tyne (George Clooney) and crew are battling the sea in a raging, gale-force storm. But they also have specific obstacles they encounter besides the overwhelming force of nature—the ship breaking down, the radio going out, interpersonal conflicts. The same is true in *Titanic*, as Rose (Kate Winslet) and Jack (Leonardo DiCaprio) struggle to survive the sinking ship as well as Hockley (Billy Zane).

Internal conflicts are the inner problems the protagonist struggles with as she tries to attain her goals. These can be emotional, psychological, or spiritual. They usually relate to what the protagonist needs to deal with in herself before she can adequately solve the primary conflict of the plot, and they help delineate the story's theme. These might be fears and neuroses. Immaturity, arrogance, and pride are all inner conflicts that a protagonist might need to overcome. In *Casablanca*, Rick's wounded ego has left him bitter and alienated from his former self. Through his interactions with Ilsa, he finally rediscovers himself. In *Jerry Maguire*, Jerry's fear of intimacy keeps him from opening up and loving Dorothy.

The struggle against destiny, fate, mystic, or supernatural forces characterizes the fourth type of obstacle. In the time of the Greeks, characters such as Oedipus and Prometheus met opposition from the gods. This was their fate. In Aeschylus's *Prometheus Bound*, Prometheus boldly places himself in direct opposition to Zeus, who is clearly an unjust, tyrannical god in this play. Or in Sophocles' *Oedipus Rex*, Oedipus's fate is foretold, and although he's honorable and tries to avoid it, he can't and ultimately brings ruin to himself and his family.

Today, we more commonly see these obstacles represented by the supernatural. Films like *The Grudge*, *The Blair Witch Project*, and *Poltergeist* all pit their heroes against nonhuman adversaries. Even *Groundhog Day* can be considered in this category. But these forces can also appear as accidents or chance or be expressed as moral choices and ethical codes. In *Erin Brockovich*, the car accident at the beginning of the film is an obstacle taking the form of a chance occurrence, literally stopping her progress and leading her to meet Ed. In *Witness*, John Book (Harrison Ford) must adhere to the Amish code while recovering on the Lapp farm. Having his gun, even as a policeman, is an obstacle to fitting in with his Amish protectors, so he hands it over to Rachel for safekeeping.

Look at any of the films mentioned and you'll see they use at least three or all four types of obstacles to create compelling plots. In *The Wizard of Oz*, Dorothy faces a personal antagonist in the Wicked Witch of the West (Margaret Hamilton), her own inner fears (internal conflicts), a bewitched forest (physical obstructions and supernatural forces), and a wizard (Frank Morgan) who refuses to help and charges her with an impossible task. When a protagonist faces only one type of obstacle, a story tends to become flat and repetitious. Compare *Jaws* with its sequels and you'll see how the subsequent films rely on one shark attack after another as obstacles to raise the conflict and how monotonous they become.

To create well-rounded plot action, physical obstacles or a persistent antagonist must take a toll on the protagonist's psyche, creating an inner turmoil for the hero. When properly conceived and presented, all obstacles force decisions on the major characters. The protagonist and antagonist must decide what they need to do and whether to do it. These decisions are the root of dramatic action.

Complications

A *complication* is any factor that enters the world of the story and causes a change in the direction of the action. Complications usually make matters worse, but they can be either positive or negative for any of the conflicting characters in the story. When a character confronts a difficult complication that demands some kind of a response, the story takes on added dimension. The action that results often forces decisions and choices on the characters that tell us about who they are.

In *The Good Girl*, Bubba (Tim Blake Nelson) sees Justine (Jennifer Aniston), his best friend's wife, with Holden (Jake Gyllenhaal) at a motel. Bubba becomes a complication when he confronts Justine about Holden and demands a price for his silence. This forces a new decision on Justine that leads to action, and it takes the story in a new direction. In *Chinatown*, when the photographs Gittes was hired to take of Mulray and the girl end up in the newspaper, this complication brings more trouble to him. The real Mrs. Mulray (Faye Dunaway) arrives and threatens to sue him, revealing that he was used. This turns the story in a new direction. Now Gittes's problem is not only professional but also personal.

The Fugitive is loaded with complications. At the end of the first act, when Kimble's on a bus heading to prison and a death sentence, a prisoner trying to escape stabs a guard in the chest. This action spirals into chaos as the bus crashes, and prisoners are killed. When the bus comes to a stop, the surviving guard commands Kimble, a doctor, to help his injured partner. The guard uncuffs Kimble's hands just before they realize that the bus has stopped on railroad tracks and a train is coming. Kimble asks the guard to help him get the hurt man out, but the uninjured man deserts him. Alone, Kimble could easily jump, but he doesn't and rescues the man, hurting himself in the process. This example of scene complications heightens the story's sense of danger and illustrates Kimball's essential character and moral code.

Complications aren't obstacles that prevent the hero from reaching his goal but other issues, problems, and difficulties he must face and manage. Complications don't pose an apparent threat to the protagonist and his goal—at least not when they initially arise. Some complications circle around in the plot to threaten your protagonist later. They can play out over several scenes but don't have to be plotted sequentially.

The best complications are unexpected—positive or negative.

Typically, complications are new characters, new developments or circumstances, mistakes, misunderstandings and—best of all—discoveries. In *Casablanca*, Rick learns that Ilsa was married when he knew her in Paris. This complicates his feelings of bitterness toward her as he realizes there may have been a real reason she had to leave him. In *Chinatown*, when Gittes discovers the truth about Mrs. Mulray and the girl, it changes the way he feels about the events and the direction he's going.

When a major complication comes in the first half of a plot, it can trigger a subplot that develops another line of action for the hero. This is how many "love interests" are introduced. In *Witness*, Book has been wounded and needs medical attention; the Amish want to take him to a hospital, but Rachel knows this would alert Book's superior to Samuel's whereabouts and threaten her son's life. Rachel fights for Book to stay and recover on the Lapp farm. This leads directly into the subplot. Book's recovery on the farm causes a closer association with her. As a result, his feelings for her grow and complicate his goal, which is to bring down the corrupt cops who are after Rachel's son and him. Rachel's feelings for him threaten her ties to her community. Both results complicate the characters' actions.

Well-placed complications contribute surprise and story extension to a plot and also offer us opportunities to reveal characters on deeper levels. The actions undertaken by characters dealing with complications help maintain tension and suspense by casting doubt on the hero's ultimate success in achieving his goal.

The Reversal

The *reversal* is the strongest action tool a writer has at her disposal. A reversal is a sudden spin of the plot action into its opposite. Positives turn to negatives, negatives to positives. The writer turns the world of her hero upside down, and with it the audience's expectations. It contributes the element of surprise to a successful plot, and this deepens audience involvement. Any bias they may have formed about the direction of the film becomes immaterial after a strong reversal, and they have to pay closer attention to what's happening to understand how the pieces all fit together.

The audience is always, to some degree, anticipating a film's plot line. Consciously or unconsciously, they try to make sense out of the events. When a film is predictable, it's unsatisfying. The use of one or two well-placed reversals in the plot will help keep the audience on its collective toes and staying with the film to its surprising finish.

Reversals can be major or minor. A major reversal spins the plot in a whole new direction while a minor reversal happens within a scene making it more interesting, fun, and unpredictable. (See any of the *Pirates of the Caribbean* films and you know what I mean.) When a character faces a major reversal, he can't go along as planned. He must deal with the unforeseen situation. This calls for new plans and actions, keeping the plot moving and the audience from guessing what will happen next. In *Witness*, the first act ends with a major reversal that changes the direction of the story from one about a good cop chasing a bad cop into bad cops pursuing a good cop.

In *Jaws*, near the midpoint of the film, we see two expertly placed major and minor reversals working together. The sequence begins with the mayor talking to a news crew and telling everyone how safe the beach is. "Amity, y'know, means friendship," he says. It's the Fourth of July and the beach is packed. People enter the water and our tension grows. When we see the fin cutting through the surf, we know we're in trouble. A swimmer reacts and everyone panics, trying to get out of the water. By the end of the sequence, it turns out to be a joke: Two boys are revealed pulling the prank. This action gives the audience a thrill but does not change the direction of the plot action. It's a perfect example of a *minor* reversal. However, if you remember the movie, the beat just following this scene shows the real shark swimming into the pond and the tension starts rising again. Here the shark kills the boater and narrowly misses Chief Brody's son. The result is that everyone sees the great white and Brody now forces the mayor in the following scene to sign the papers that hire Quint (Robert Shaw). This drives the plot in its final direction, toward the confrontation between the men and the shark.

Reversals can come anywhere in a plot, but major reversals come most often at the key structural points: the first act climax, the midpoint, and the second and the third act climaxes. They're very effective at these story junctures because they demand a response from the main characters and lead to action in a new and unexpected direction. The reversal in *Jaws* cited above comes at the midpoint, moving Chief Brody's main conflict in the first half of the film with the town elders into a direct confrontation with the shark.

Reversals don't magically appear when you're outlining your story. The best twists are plotted. That means you're consciously designing sequences to surprise your audience. You need to think of what the audience expects to happen and then create the exact opposite or work to misdirect them, to intentionally get them expecting one outcome while you are plotting the opposite. In *Risky Business*, Miles (Curtis Armstrong), the Harvard-bound friend, calls a hooker and destroys the number before Joel (Tom Cruise) can stop him. We're expecting a beautiful young woman to appear. When Jackie (Bruce A. Young), the clearly male transvestite, materializes, we're as surprised as Joel. How Joel resolves the conflict with Jackie leads to him getting Lana's number (Rebecca De Mornay) and sets up the real story.

In the first act of *Quiz Show*, a modern-day Faustian story about the scandal surrounding the late 1950s TV game show *21*, Stempel (John Turturro) has been told by Enright (David Paymer) to lose on the "Marty" question. Stempel's wife (Johann Carlo) urges him to answer correctly—why should he have to take a fall? It looks like Stempel will play it his way. The audience knows about his collusion with Enright, but what can Enright really do to him? However, when the moment of truth comes, Stempel does exactly what Enright told him to do; he loses, setting up Charlie (Ralph Fiennes) for his win. In the second act, Stempel's jealousy over Charlie's success increases. Obsessed with bringing Charlie down, Stempel admits to Goodwin (Rob Morrow) that he cheated and got the answers from Enright all along. This information shocks Goodwin and reverses his course; now he goes after Charlie, and this leads us into the third act.

Reversals don't just change the direction of the story. They have emotional repercussions, too, moving characters from hope to despair or from sadness to joy, as they react to their sudden change of circumstances. The audience feels the emotions with the characters, drawing viewers deeper into the story.

CHARACTER TOOLS

One of the biggest criticisms writers, both novice and experienced, get is that the protagonists and other characters in their screenplays are flat and uninteresting. In screenwriting, the focus is on action in plotting, what a character is doing, and not on a narrative that can include prose to explain a character's background, motivations, and desires. We must find ways that expose the character's inner workings in action to make our points about her. This isn't to say writers don't include scenes that give exposition about who the characters are; it's just that these scenes are not usually very effective.

Characters in movies must come alive and be revealed in what they do more than in what they say. Yet, even successful screenwriters resort to dialogue that explains some aspect of the character. In *Jerry Maguire*, Cameron Crowe gives us scenes in early drafts of the script that tell us about Jerry's home life growing up. None of these scenes makes it into the movie. In *Chinatown*, an early draft of Robert Towne's script gives us a four-page scene in which Gittes explains the meaning of "Chinatown" to Evelyn. In the movie, this dialogue gets reduced to about three lines: There was a girl, I couldn't save her, it was Chinatown. In both cases, the filmmakers knew the information, although necessary to the author to understand the characters, was not necessary to the audience to understand the story. The protagonists had revealed more about who they were through their actions than the exposition explaining particular backgrounds had added, therefore making this information extraneous as well as dangerous to the stories' momentum.

Obviously, what a character tells us about himself (and what other characters say about him) counts and is necessary, but explanation is no substitute for action in film. Drama is character in action. Characters develop in the course of a story in accordance with the historical present of the plot. It is a twofold development: first showing how the characters are shaped by the events in which they're involved, and second, presenting them progressively to the audience. The key to creating compelling characters in film is to find the revealing *actions that describe who a character is*. Character tools help us pinpoint and use these actions. They expose characters' motivations, feelings, and thinking and, at the deepest level, their essence.

Before I start defining these tools for revealing your characters, I'd like to talk a moment about what makes a strong protagonist.

Every screenwriting book on the market talks about how the protagonist must have a goal, something she wants. The goal/want/desire draws the protagonist toward something, giving her something to pursue, and so drives the action of the plot. Dramas evolve from characters in action and in conflict with one another, and an audience instinctively gravitates toward a character or group of characters striving to attain a goal. (Active characters are more interesting and sympathetic than passive characters, even if good-guy/bad-guy roles are reversed. A trapped character who complains and takes no action is boring.)

But to consider this driving action just movement toward a goal doesn't do it justice. The question arises: Why, when the going gets tough, doesn't the protagonist just walk away from the film? If the protagonist is trapped in the situation, like Rose and Jack in *Titanic*, Billy Tyne and Bobby Shatford (Mark Wahlberg) in *The Perfect Storm*, or Shawn (Simon Pegg) and Ed (Nick Frost) in *Shawn of the Dead*, then obviously he can't. But many scripts don't go this far, and as we read on we wonder what's driving the character to continue.

Protagonists Make Commitments

A goal must represent a major commitment for the protagonist. Your protagonist must be committed to something—her goal, a value system, a person, etc.—and be willing to fight for it, even die. Her action in the film becomes a test of her commitment and the price she's willing to pay for maintaining or forsaking it. Look at the lengths Will Turner in *Pirates of the Caribbean* will go to for the people in his life he makes commitments to. He lays his life on the line for Elizabeth, Jack, and his father, time and again. The audience cares about Will because *they care about characters who make commitments, especially to other people.*

Great writers know the significant action a character takes should both cost and gain him something valuable. In *Munich*, Avner (Eric Bana) is committed to Israel and agrees to lead a group of Mossad agents to track down and kill the terrorists who murdered Israel's Olympic athletes. This is his goal. As he acts to achieve this, the brutality of the murders exacts a toll on him. By the end of the film, the personal cost of the ordeal has been his humanity. This is the consequence of the action taken.

With this in mind, remember that a sense of personal loss is best expressed in the context of relationships. Hamlet loses Ophelia because of his determination to kill his uncle; Mark Anthony forsakes his honor and Roman privileges for Cleopatra's love. Rick in *Casablanca* gives up Ilsa to fight for the greater good; Jerry in *Jerry Maguire* loses all of his other clients because of his determination to hold Rod.

Conflict Reveals Character

The first character tool is your character's reactions to the important moments of conflict and conflict resolution in your story. Understand that conflict strips away our masks and defenses. The *only* way a character shows us who she really is, what her *character* is made of, is how she deals with conflict. In *The Art of Dramatic Writing*, Lajos Egri wrote that only in conflict do we reveal our true selves. "Even an illiterate knows that politeness and smart talk are not signs of sincerity or friendship. But sacrifice is."

How we react to trouble tells us about our essential selves. Do we fall apart in the face of misfortune or buckle down and work harder? Do we sweep our problems under the rug or chin up and face them? When trouble comes calling, do we run for fear we'll be hurt or stand up and fight for what's right? Is our perspective "What will happen to me?" or "What can I get done?"

Character, the kind that excites readers, actors, and audiences, is not a laundry list of qualities and traits, a biography of where Johnny grew up and whether Mommy loved him or not. This is the psychology of the character. (All this is important information for the writer but is of little consequence to the audience if they "get" what the character is about on an emotional level.) Character, in the dramatic sense, is shown in the strengths and weaknesses of the personality that we see *dramatized in action* on-screen.

This is what great screenwriters know: Stories aren't about a situation or a series of actions; they're about characters caught in conflict over a commitment, reacting to the situations at hand in ways that the audience finds compelling, identifiable, and understandable. A character has a (back) story but he is *not* that (back) story. Indeed, we could argue that the purpose of drama is to demonstrate how (heroic) people take action that is outside the realm of their personality. We show how people change or alter their basic psychology when they realize their usual patterns of behavior will get them killed, literally or figuratively. (Comedies, of course, or wistful dramas like *Forrest Gump*, or fantasies like the 007 series, are often built around the premise that a "hero" will change his circumstances despite never having to undergo change himself.)

What do we know of Lester Burnham in *American Beauty*? He's a frustrated middle-aged man who hates his life. We don't get a life history that tells us why he's this way; we see it demonstrated in his actions and through the conflict with his wife, daughter, and the external world. He's so sexually frustrated he obsesses over his daughter's friend Angela, and this raises the stakes of the story. Yet how and why do we connect with him?

Even as we squirm while he makes a fool of himself with Angela and strains his relationship with his daughter, we admire his courage for confronting the job he hates and turning the bad situation to his advantage by securing a hefty severance package. We see in his emotional reactions regret over angry words he exchanges with his daughter. We feel his longing and frustration with his wife when she can't give an inch. And in the end, as he recognizes Angela's vulnerability and puts her needs above his own desires, we see in his actions his core humanity. This is why Lester is a great character and an Oscar-worthy role.

Decisions and Choices

The best stories capture characters in situations where they are called on to make tough decisions and choices, ones with real consequences, the more moral the better. Spider-Man, Lester Burnham, Will Turner and Elizabeth Swann, and Jerry Maguire and Dorothy Boyd are all characters faced with hard choices in difficult situations. We know what's in their hearts from ancillary action and exposition. But we learn the extent to which they will make a moral choice, even if it breaks their hearts, by the action they undertake.

Great writers understand that making a difficult decision or choice is dramatic action. They dramatize the situations that place their characters at the blazing crossroads of choice and then rake them over the coals to turn their actions into significant moments of the plot.

First, let's distinguish the difference between decisions and choices in drama. A *decision* is the process of coming to a conclusion about something. It is a judgment about possibilities and a making up of your mind about what to do. A *choice* is a decision, too, but is more specific and often considered dramatically more productive because it is a voluntary act of selecting or separating from two or more things that which is preferred, offering a character radically different outcomes. A choice has a cost, something the character forsakes or sacrifices in order to get what he wants. For example, it's too easy if Superman has no choice but to save the school. But if he has to choose between the lives of many children and that of Lois Lane, things get tougher. The best way to frame these choices is in moral terms, but not in moral absolutes. Let the audience see the character struggle with the moral dilemma of acting for oneself or for others, and it brings a deeper complexity to the plot than proselytizing for one form of action over another.

In drama, we need to find the key decisions and choices a character makes. They will lead to decisive action and draw a reaction. Often feature films and scripts gloss over the process of coming to a decision or making a choice because writers and filmmakers are afraid it will slow or stall the action. But making a decision *is* an action. It is the decision to act or not to act that can help us understand who that character is fundamentally, revealing his thoughts and motivations.

Think about the first *Spider-Man*. It's loaded with decisions and choices. Peter thinks a car will help him win M.J., so he decides to go to Wrestle-mania and compete as "The Human Spider." He beats his opponent, but the wrestling promoter cheats him out of his winnings. When a robber appears, Peter is faced with a choice: He can help the promoter who cheated him or not. Peter chooses not to help, and the robber gets away. Then Peter discovers Uncle Ben has been murdered in a carjacking. Peter reacts and goes after the killer. He tracks the carjacker down and realizes the man who robbed Wrestle-mania, the man he let go, is Uncle Ben's killer. The consequences of Peter's actions hit him. This takes him to his next choice: whether to kill the man or let the police get him. The filmmakers push the villain here to force Peter's hand in his death, but his action, his choice, tells us who he has become. In the scene following his high school graduation, we see the clear decision Peter makes to accept responsibility for his powers and become Spider-Man. If you view this scene, you'll see how the filmmakers hit the emotion of the decision to make the audience feel it even more with Peter.

The process of deciding and choosing between options can heighten the drama and suspense while we await the action that shows what's going on inside the character. Playing these moments also allows the audience the chance to process with the characters what's happening, giving viewers time to feel what the characters feel to deepen the bond between them. New writers often offer characters choices between something positive (e.g., the man the protagonist really loves) and something negative (e.g., a man she'll never love). But this isn't really a choice. It doesn't lead to sacrifice. Unless it's Luke Skywalker choosing between the good on the side of the rebels or standing with his father and the evil Empire, it is dramatically ineffective because the negative doesn't represent something the character truly wants.

Consider the choice Roy Neary (Richard Dreyfuss) makes in *Close Encounters of the Third Kind*. Leaving his wife and family seems like the only sane thing to do because she is such a shrew, and the call of the unknown is so powerful. Because we don't care if he stays, the impact of his choice is weakened. We want him to go. What if, however, Roy had a sick child and the choice was to stay and help the family or go fulfill his destiny and follow the flying saucers? The stakes get higher, his choice becomes less automatic, more moral (whatever he chooses), and his need (to see other worlds) is more vividly demonstrated.

Choices and decisions are strongest when they have consequences. When the mildly maladjusted Elliot in *E.T.: The Extra-Terrestrial* realizes he must let his one good friend, E.T., go home, he's made a difficult moral choice, a sacrifice. Because we understand how much this choice will cost Elliot, we buy how hard he will work to keep E.T. from the government's clutches. In *Pulp Fiction*, Butch (Bruce Willis) manages to free himself from the hands of the rapists while they're occupied with Marcellus (Ving Rhames). Butch makes it all the way to the door and freedom, but he can't leave. He makes a choice and risks his life—for the man who wants to kill him. Why? Because walking away would go against his own moral code.

Chief Brody in *Jaws* gives in to mayoral requests to keep the beach open, and bathers die as a result. The chief chose wrong: He sided with the mayor and against the scientist, and the guilt over this choice, with a desire to avenge the deaths of swimmers by killing the shark, will motivate him for the rest of the story. There's a child's blood on his hands now, the hands of a lawman, a family man, a man who never really liked the water—the place where his adversary lies. But he's going after the fish; he must act. He's doing so under extreme pressure with a real moral imperative (to protect innocent life), against a literally cold-blooded, amoral antagonist. Who's going to stop reading or watching him now?

Choices and Reversals

For writers creating an exciting plot, another helpful aspect about the act of choosing is how the choice can be used to set up a reversal. A character is presented with a choice. His actions demonstrate which option he'd prefer; however, the undesirable alternative still holds value for him. The audience sees the protagonist struggle and then commit to a course of action toward what he wants, refusing the other option, until the last moment when a change of heart occurs. The character chooses the alternative he didn't want, but for a reason the audience understands.

In *Five Easy Pieces*, Bobby (Jack Nicholson) is a man at odds with himself, and just about everybody else around him. The first part of the film shows him as an unpredictable guy, working in the oil fields, living with his waitress girlfriend, Rayette (Karen Black), and unable to make or keep a commitment. His relationship with

Rayette is more about convenience than love. Around twenty minutes into the film, just after Bobby's discovers Rayette is pregnant, Bobby leaves the oil fields of Bakersfield for a Los Angeles recording studio where he meets his sister (Lois Smith), a concert pianist. She reveals that their father is sick and Bobby must come home. Now the audience learns Bobby isn't an oil roughneck by birth but from an entirely different class. He takes the news dutifully and returns to Bakersfield.

When Bobby arrives at his place, he finds Rayette curled up in his bed, incommunicado. He tries to engage her, but she refuses to talk to him and he gets angry. He flat out tells her he has to go home; his father is sick. He'll be gone two or three weeks. But Rayette knows he'll just leave her and their affair will be over. While packing, he softens some and tells her he'll try to call, but this makes no difference to her. She weeps soundlessly, unable to face him. Finally, he heads toward the door and says, "Come on, DiPesto. I never told you it would work out to anything. Did I?" When she still won't respond, he utters a few more empty phrases and then leaves.

In front of the house, Bobby slams the suitcase into the backseat of his beat-up car. He climbs behind the wheel and sits for a moment before he turns the ignition. Then suddenly, he flips out, cursing himself and her as he slams the steering wheel. A second later, he storms out of the car. In the next beat, Bobby's back in the house and he asks Rayette, "Do you want to come with me?" The scene ends on her smile.

During the scene, Bobby is committed to leaving without Rayette. From his actions previous to these scenes, the audience knows that he doesn't place that much value on this relationship. They've seen him treat Rayette badly and cheat on her. But by the end of this scene, when he comes in and asks Rayette to go with him, the audience learns that he must care about her. Clearly, he's acting on her behalf more than on his. The audience reads the scene that he doesn't want to hurt her. By the end of the movie, they might have a different interpretation of these events, but for now, his actions surprise and impress them. Dramatically, the scene is much more exciting because of the conflict between the characters, and the end of it, with the twist, provides a surprise, both in terms of the plot *and* the character.

Structurally Effective Choices and Decisions

Decisions and choices can come anywhere in a film's plot. But major decisions and choices are most effective when played at the film's structural turning points. When choices are played at the first-, second-, and third-act climaxes, and the midpoint, they clarify the focus and meaning of the action, crystallize the stakes by providing clear consequences to the action, and show us who the characters are via what they choose.

In *The Matrix*, will Neo take the red pill or the blue pill (end of act one)? In *Quiz Show*, will Charlie (Ralph Fiennes) answer the question and take Enright's bait (David Paymer) or expose the sham (end of act one)? These choices define the characters as well as the direction of the action. In *Quiz Show*, as a result of Charlie's falling prey to Enright's temptation, he goes from being an anonymous adjunct professor at Columbia to a national icon. In *The Matrix*, Neo takes the red pill and the adventure begins. Both these decisions lead to actions that take their plots into the second act.

In *The Good Girl*, will Justine (Jennifer Aniston) turn Holden (Jake Gyllenhaal) in or not (act two climax)? In *Catch Me If You Can*, will Frank (Leonardo DiCaprio) believe Carl's (Tom Hanks) story about the French police wanting to kill him and escape under Carl's protection or will he walk out that door alone, without being handcuffed, and risk being shot (act two climax)? In *The Devil Wears Prada*, will Andy (Anne Hathaway) choose Miranda

Priestly's (Meryl Streep) life or her own (the climax)? In *Roman Holiday*, will Anne (Audrey Hepburn) stay with Joe (Gregory Peck) or return to the throne (the climax)? These choices, coming at crucial points in the plot, show us the essence of the characters by the end of the film.

Making characters decide or choose gives them more dimension and life. It allows you to illustrate who they are by these decisions and choices, instead of you conceiving them as a consolidation of back-story and already-made judgments that really have more to do with attitude than action.

Revelation

Another character tool, which can also be an exposition tool, is the *revelation*. Revelation is key information the audience and characters need to understand the full extent of the story. It comes as a shock or surprise, but always makes sense, shedding light on one of the main characters or plot elements. Now the audience understands why actions were taken, despite the risks. Sometimes revelation is an epiphany the protagonist has about his life as a result of the events experienced in the film. Often it's information that has a direct bearing on the protagonist's goals.

Because *Chinatown* is a detective story, information is always coming to light. But when the revelation takes place, the story takes on a whole new meaning. Gittes enters the scene believing Evelyn's guilty of murdering her husband. He is intent on forcing a confession out of her to save his detective's license. He confronts her and demands the identity of the girl who has been at the heart of his case and whom he knows Evelyn is harboring. "She's my daughter," she says finally, and Gittes snaps. He slaps her hard and asks again. "She's my sister." He hits her again and again, until finally Evelyn reveals, "She's my sister *and* my daughter." With this revelation, everything changes, for Gittes and the audience. Gittes, who starts this scene ready to turn Evelyn in, now reverses course and will do whatever he can to save her.

In *Casablanca*, at the midpoint of the film, Ilsa reveals to Rick that when she knew him in Paris she was already married to Laszlo. This is his first indication there may have been a bona fide reason why she had to leave him. At the end of act two, Ilsa reveals the whole story of her exit from Paris. Her explanation frees him from his passivity and allows him to act.

When revelation is specifically a character's epiphany, it's best when it's shown through action. We either peer into the true heart of the protagonist (or other character) as he reveals himself or see it directly in his interactions with other characters. *American Beauty* shows Lester's core self through his interaction with Angela at the climax of the film. In *Jerry Maguire*, Jerry realizes at the climax he wants Dorothy and rushes off to win her back. This is not so much a secret the character has been keeping but a new realization the character has achieved.

A common mistake new writers make when playing a revelation is to expose it too easily. Someone asks a question, or a character volunteers it. But in great films, revelation is forced out through conflict. It isn't just handed over willy-nilly. Characters don't want to reveal their secrets, and only do so because they must. Look at how Gittes forces Evelyn to confess her deepest secret through physical confrontation. Or examine *North by Northwest*, and the revelation that Eve Kendall (Eva Marie Saint) is *not* Vandamm's (James Mason) mistress but a double agent. No one wants this information to be exposed, especially the professor (Leo G. Carroll), but it's forced out because of the feelings between Eve and Thornhill (Cary Grant), and because everything the government wanted from this charade is now at risk.

This brings us to another aspect of the revelation. It frequently leads to a reverse in the direction of the plot action. In *North by Northwest*, Thornhill switches directions once he learns Eve's true identity and acts to help the government get Vandamm. In the examples above from *Chinatown* and *Casablanca*, we see the story reversals alongside the revelations.

Revelations most often take place in the second half of a plot and are more powerful when linked with other elements like reversals, crises, and turning points or act climaxes. The main revelation usually occurs near the climax of the second act, although it can come as early as the first act to start the story off with a bang, or at the third act climax. *Witness* ends the first act with the revelation that Book's superior, Schaeffer, is part of the murder he's investigating. This revelation/reversal turns the plot in a new direction and pumps the drama. Wherever it comes, a revelation tends to act as a catalyst and propel the plot into the next portion of the film.

A strong revelation always has consequences, frequently drastic. Sometimes the startling information causes the protagonist to doubt himself before he finds the strength to recommit to the goal and story. Or it confirms the protagonist's struggle, sending him and the film rushing toward its conclusion. Seeing these responses dramatized allows the audience a glimpse of the protagonist's true character.

EXPOSITION TOOLS

As with revelations, exposition tools enlighten us to certain aspects of the story by revealing information the audience needs to follow along. All films have a certain amount of information that must be worked into the plot, especially in the beginning, so that the audience is oriented to the story's direction and understands what's happening. At the beginning this is referred to as the *main exposition*. It's concerned with place, establishing the main characters and their relationships, and setting up the main conflict.

But exposition really continues throughout a film. Essentially, a plot is all information. As you structure the plot action, you're managing it to tell the story in its most effective form. We see some of the information dramatized through characters' actions and interactions, through how they meet the conflict and its effect. But there is other information that has to be clearly stated, in words or pictures. If your audience doesn't understand what's happening, if they can't follow along and make the connections in the action, they can't follow the film.

Here are a few ways to help get the exposition across.

The Main Exposition

The audience can't pay intelligent attention to a story if it's not first acquainted with the previous circumstances on which the story is based. The *main exposition* is the information the audience needs at the start of the film to understand the story that develops. It should look backward in time no more than it must. When *North by Northwest* starts, all we know is that Roger O. Thornhill is a hapless New York advertising executive mistakenly identified as George Kaplan, a spy. He's thrown into the middle of intrigue with the same amount of information as we have, and we're able to follow along quite nicely. In *Jerry Maguire*, the main exposition is carried by narration and action that covers a great deal of information about where Jerry is in his life right now: in a personal crisis. Writer Cameron Crowe tells and dramatizes all the background we need to understand the story that develops.

The initial exposition in a solid film is brief and to the point, making clear whatever is not self-explanatory. Many writers either give too much information at the start of their scripts or too little.

If there's too much, it takes too long for the conflict to heat up and the reader gets bored. If there's too little, the reader doesn't have enough information to grasp the important ideas and gets lost. Either way spells disaster.

The Plan

Once the conflict has been introduced to the protagonist, he usually comes up with the *plan* of action. The plan shows how the protagonist initially grasps the problem and what he intends to do about it. It suggests the direction he'll follow. It most often shows up in dialogue, helping to specifically orient the audience to the problem and the character's intention toward it.

Plans come up in the beginning of a plot and then recur as characters meet with resistance and have to form new plans to attain their goals. As the story progresses, there is often a disparity between the protagonist's anticipated results and the reality represented by the conflict the hero continues to encounter. The protagonist's action leads him to bump his head up against the wall, until he comes up with a new plan. When the action swings in a new and unexpected direction as a result of difficulties, this produces both surprise and more tension.

The plan is both an exposition tool and an action tool. It gives us exposition by allowing the hero to state his position with regard to his goal; it leads to action when we see the protagonist implementing his plan. In *Jerry Maguire,* Jerry's plan of action is his Mission Statement he distributes to his colleagues, describing how to be successful and human in a dog-eat-dog world. Instead of this leading to success, Jerry winds up losing his job.

Plans can be carefully thought out or moment-to-moment. In *Erin Brockovich*, Erin and Ed make plans regarding the case throughout the movie. We see their reasoning and understand their positions and intentions. In *Field Of Dreams*, Ray Kinsella's (Kevin Costner) plan is totally eclectic and moment-to-moment; he's following a voice he hears in a cornfield.

Narration

Right now narration is in vogue to help take care of exposition. Films like *Little Children, Stranger than Fiction, Adaptation,* and *The Hours* have all shown how effective it can be. The problem is that most scripts don't use it creatively. It's simply there to tell us what's going on, or worse, it tells what we already know from the plot action. Used either way, it renders the action flat and boring and kills the subtext of scenes. There is nothing for the viewer to figure out because it's all been handed over.

For narration to work well, it has to have a specific voice and add another dimension to the story. In *American Beauty*, the narration has an ironic tone that foreshadows conflict. It shapes as well as relays information but is used sparingly. In *The Hours*, the narration provides information as well as continuity in connecting the three separate story lines. Both *Little Children* and *Stranger than Fiction* use narration similarly. Each one uses irony and insight to creatively tell the story. But where *Little Children* uses narration to add to our knowledge of the plot line, *Stranger than Fiction* turns the narrating voice into a specific character that not only tells the story but also creates major conflict for Harold. *Adaptation* uses narration as comic relief, exposing Charlie Kaufman's (Nicholas Cage) inner conflicts and making us laugh. It often contrasts what we see. *Annie Hall* does the same thing, and so does *About Schmidt*, through the letters Warren (Jack Nicholson) writes to his "adopted" child in Africa.

Jerry Maguire, Field of Dreams, and *The Piano* all use initial narration to set tone and deliver important information the audience needs to start the film. *Field of Dreams* does it in a straightforward fashion, while in *Jerry Maguire* and *The Piano* it's just as direct but fraught with conflict.

Written cards serve the same purpose. These are just what they sound like, written information the audience must read before it leaves the screen. They easily express details and are often used at the beginning, helping to clarify the main exposition and draw the audience into the film. In *Shakespeare in Love*, a written card over a black screen tells us at the start where we are, London, England, 1593. Another card appears: "In the glory days of the Elizabethan theatre two playhouses were fighting it out for writers and audiences. North of the city was the Curtain Theatre, home to England's most famous actor, Richard Burbage." Then as the picture fades in, introducing the stage, the words continue: "Across the river was the competition, built by Philip Henslowe, a business with a cash flow problem...The Rose..." Now the audience is oriented to where they are and ready for the film to start. In *Star Wars: A New Hope*, the crawl at the beginning establishes the conflict between the resistance and the Empire, grounding the audience in the opposition at the root of the story.

Exposition presented this way usually comes at the start of a film to help set the scene, but it can work from beginning to end, too. Don Roos's film *Happy Endings* uses written cards throughout to add information and comment on the plot action, mostly to good effect.

Written information can be a powerful tool for a writer because the moment it comes on the screen the audience needs to start paying close attention, and they usually do for fear of missing something important. But the danger is always that the writer will tell too much, drowning the audience in information instead of dramatizing a story.

Minor Conflicts

Minor conflicts are just what they seem: conflicts of lesser importance used to make getting information across more interesting. Often these conflicts undulate through a plot, creating continuity through the characters as well as adding to the tension.

Pintel (Lee Arenberg) and Ragetti (Mackenzie Crook) in the *Pirates of the Caribbean* films squabble over everything as information is laid out for the audience. Henslowe (Geoffrey Rush) and Fennyman (Tom Wilkinson) in *Shakespeare in Love* bicker over the details of putting on the play while they tell the audience what's going on. Miles in *Risky Business* is constantly on Joel's case as they deliver exposition to get the story going. Jeff (Bill Murray) in *Tootsie* argues with his roommate Michael (Dustin Hoffman) over Dorothy's interference in their lives. This conflict makes getting Michael's plans across to the audience more entertaining.

Remember: Conflict makes people pay attention. When you want them to retain information, using conflict is one of the best ways to drive a point home.

Visual Information

Visual information consists of specific visual details that help the audience understand what they need to know in the plot. In *Spider-Man*, not only are there spiders everywhere in the university lab, but a looping presentation on a video screen in the background shows DNA strands and the project title: "Genetic Research." When the spider escapes its terrarium the audience knows it's dangerous. Remember how the estate in *Shakespeare in Love* dwarfs the characters the first time we see it from the outside. It contrasts the squalid digs Will lives in and lets viewers see Viola's (Gwyneth Paltrow) wealth.

Consider carefully in your descriptions what you want the reader and then the viewer to learn from the backdrops of your scenes. What is in a character's room, for example, can tell a lot about whom that character is. Actions and behavior are good, too. How unforgettable is Melvin Udall (Jack Nicholson) in *As Good As It Gets* walking down the sidewalk without stepping on cracks? That's what you're looking for in your scenes.

CHAPTER 6

THE SEQUENCE OF STORY

In a plot's organization of scenes, action and emotion must be effectively managed for the audience to follow the flow of information, maintain interest, and understand the ultimate meaning of the story. This information consists of the setting, exposition, main and secondary characters, rising action, main conflict, subconflicts in obstacles and complications, subplots, emotional reactions, and more. It's a lot to manage. And it's one of the reasons most scripts are so confused. When plots jump around from scene to scene, main conflict to subplot, and information byte to information byte, audiences (readers and viewers) tend to become frustrated because it's harder for them to make the connections between the scenes and therefore understand what it all means. They're given a piece of information here about one aspect of the story, then another piece about a different aspect, and then another...and it all just feels like a jumble. But this is how many new writers' scripts read.

For a film to work, it needs to adhere to the principles of drama so that information is conveyed in such a way that the audience can track it through action, visuals, and sound. Structure is the first organizational tactic a writer uses to ensure this. It creates a framework to manage and make sense of all the material. But it's only the first step.

Plotting a story is creating a sequence of events that moves seemingly effortlessly from one scene to the next, guiding the reader first, and then hopefully the viewer, through the complex interplay of elements to tell the tale. Plotting turns the structural story considerations that have to do with conflict and meaning into moments that convey exposition, build suspense, reveal character, and expose emotion in ways that deepen the audience's involvement. It takes the structural framing points and finds the most interesting, surprising, and moving ways to connect them. Plotting is really the art of creating the relationships between your scenes to make your story points more powerful and meaningful. (By "story points" I mean more than just "turning" or "plot" points and act breaks; I mean the important information, emotion, and action of a story.)

I once had a student who conceived an intriguing psychological horror story but the end product didn't work. You couldn't sense the characters, motivations were fuzzy, and so much was happening that the story got lost. When faced with my comments, the writer bristled. She pointed to scenes in the script that were designed specifically to show different sides of the character. To her the protagonist *was* real and fleshed out, and the story moved.

Why these scenes didn't resonate and leave the effect she wanted on the reader was because they weren't dramatically connected by specific cause-and-effect actions. She didn't dramatize the particular characteristics of her protagonist in terms of actions and responses. The reader couldn't understand the character's motivations or track the important clues of the story. *The scenes didn't build in a chain of events to make the important points*. The writer had conceived a story in her mind but hadn't found a way to illustrate it in terms of cause-and-effect scene relationships for her characters.

She isn't unique. Many new writers don't understand that *film stories are best told in terms of cause-and-effect sequences*, not in individual scenes that convey a point and then move on to the next scene. When writers work in the "separate scene" modus, they often have a lot of action and events, but very little is conveyed in it about the characters. Their scripts are often criticized as flat and/or confusing, even though the writer may point to scenes he thought added dimension. Readers often miss these scenes because they aren't dramatized with cause-and-effect connections. The information leaves little impact on the reader and so fades into the background with all the lesser details.

THE OUTLINE OF EVENTS

This problem often begins in the outlining stage. Many of us approach writing a screenplay as a process of connecting sixty or so scenes in a line from beginning to end and outline with this in mind. We see the story as a string of individual incidents that together convey the action and conflict. They take us from a beginning and leave us at an end. (This number sixty comes from an old screenwriting standard that takes the average scene as two pages, and sixty scenes make 120 pages. Today the average scene is about 1 3/4 pages, but it's just too hard to calculate that quickly, so we still round the number off at two.)

The problem is that writers tend to view these individual scenes as separate ideas. These sixty to seventy scenes *all* contain important information. Screenplays are jammed and overcomplicated because of it. With so much going on there isn't time to develop the ideas properly for the characters and show what the events mean to them. A writer might include in an outline action that seems to take place in one location, and have a beginning, middle, and end, but to be effective the action should move through several locales and take more time.

For instance, a writer, in scene one of her outline, introduced her protagonist on a seaplane getting stoned with a pilot, landing, grabbing a cab and joking around with the driver, and rushing home and feeling like a failure. Obviously, this was not one scene, but many. Because she couldn't focus her major idea to dramatize over several scenes, her sixty-scene outline was so engorged with information in each scene that to write it properly would have doubled the length of the script. Instead, she tried to jam everything into 120 pages, resulting in a screenplay that rushed through the events. Readers had a hard time connecting with her character and keeping track of what was important to the story. When stories jump from scene to scene and the connections between them aren't clear, the significance of the ideas is lost on the reader who doesn't know where to focus.

FEATURE FILMS ARE STRUCTURED IN GROUPS OF SCENES

Great films effectively manage their story information by breaking the plot down into well-developed *segments*. These segments focus the line of action for the viewer so he can see and follow a progression of events in the escalating conflict and the characters' responses. There are strong cause-and-effect relationships between the scenes, each one building on the preceding ones and leading to the next. Each segment has a specific bearing on the main plot. Even if it veers off the main plot line and picks up a subplot or focuses on characterization, its meaning will become clear by the end.

Feature films have between eighteen and twenty-five main ideas that develop into as many as sixty to seventy scenes (give or take a few). The basis of most stories is relatively simple but well developed. These ideas are organized into groups of scenes that build and develop the important ideas. This allows the writer to give a main idea enough time and weight for the audience to track and understand its importance to the story.

Structural Considerations

The key here is to understand how strong story structure serves as the foundation for effective plotting when the causal relationships between the main focal points of each act are clear. Because of the countless books already devoted to this elusive topic, my review here is brief and only concerned with basic organizational strategies. For more on this subject, see *Secrets of Screenplay Structure*.

Structure in its simplest form has a beginning, middle, and an end. Specific genres have certain requirements that further define the structure of their stories, but this plan is flexible enough to encompass them all. The purpose of the first act is to set up the characters and the main conflict (along with the important points relating to them) and raise the dramatic question of the film. The second act focuses on the rising action in the confrontation between the opposing forces and the ensuing complications. The third act resolves the oppositions and creates the final meaning.

Act One

Your main structural points of the first act include the opening, the inciting incident, and the act one climax. The opening of the first act sets the main exposition, the information about the story the audience needs to know to understand the conflict that follows. It then builds to the inciting incident. Linda Seger, in her book *Making a Good Script Great*, calls this the catalyst, and that's exactly what it is: Something happens that demands a response from the protagonist and pushes the story to develop. At the first act climax, the main problem or conflict is clearly declared, and action must result from it.

In genre pieces, the action is closely described by the plot problem. In *Se7en*, a police procedural, the narrative action details the problem of the serial killer and its effect on the protagonists. The opening introduces Somerset, a detective at the end of his rope, retiring in seven days. He has to train his replacement, Mills, a young man new to the city who Somerset clearly thinks is crazy for wanting his job. The first murder functions as the inciting incident. Although they don't yet know what's at stake, this starts the investigation. Conflict builds between Somerset and Mills, and the captain (R. Lee Ermey) reassigns the younger detective to a second murder, effectively splitting them up. At the end of the first act, Somerset connects the two crimes. As a result, he walks off the case, leaving it to Mills. This declares the real conflict of the film and raises the dramatic question it will pursue: Can the police catch the serial killer?

In a drama such as *American Beauty*, we see a similar setup. The opening of *American Beauty* establishes the possibility of murder and then announces it with Lester's voiceover telling the audience that he'll be dead within a year. Expository dialogue says it clearly: "In a way, I'm dead already." This is an unhappy family. He and his wife, Carolyn, don't get along on any level; and their daughter clearly can't stand either one of them. The inciting incident at the basketball game introduces Lester's obsession with Angela. She makes him feel alive, and this infatuation threatens his family relationships even more. Lester goes through the motions of his marriage, accompanying Carolyn to her real estate banquet, where he meets his new neighbor Ricky and Carolyn snares a lunch with Buddy Kane. But the end of the first act builds on Lester's infatuation with Angela; he overhears Angela tell his daughter Jane she thinks he's cute. She might sleep with him if Lester lost some weight and started working out. And this is just what Lester starts doing. This is the real impetus for Lester to change his life—but at the risk of alienating everyone else in it. His action raises the dramatic questions: Will Lester act on his impulses toward the girl, and what will happen as a result of it?

We can see from these two diverse examples that the first act clearly defines the problem for the characters and the initial stakes. In *Se7en*, innocent lives are at stake; in *American Beauty*, it's Lester's relationship with his family. In each, we can see the connections between the main focal points of the first act, and that it climaxes in such a way as to demand a response from the characters that will drive the second act. In *Se7en* we have a protagonist who is supposed to be training (i.e., mentoring) his replacement. They investigate the first murder at the inciting incident. At the climax of the first act, Somerset realizes it's the work of a serial killer and leaves the case to Mills. In *American Beauty*, Lester feels dead at the opening; by the inciting incident, he feels alive. At the end of the first act, he acts alive.

Act Two

Act two centers around the confrontation with the problem and complications that arise with it, building the rising action. The setup for this confrontation is based on what happens at the end of the first act but still needs to build, usually with new information in the form of new developments. Complications can be twofold: They can be independent of the main conflict and just make things more difficult, or they often result from how the conflict affects the protagonist and other main characters. The *midpoint* serves as the focal point of the first half of act two, and the outcome of whatever happens here drives the action toward the second act climax.

In *Se7en*, the first half of the action in act two is driven by the second and third crimes. Once Mills's wife (Gwyneth Paltrow) intercedes and brings Somerset back on the case, the detectives find the handprints behind the painting in "Greed's" office. They believe they're onto their man. The two detectives identify the suspect and then follow along with the SWAT team to get him, all the while feeling uneasy. Instead of producing their man, this action leads to the third crime scene and more frustration. But throughout this action, the relationship between Somerset and Mills strengthens; as different as both men are, each is good at his job and earns the other's respect. Near the midpoint Somerset decides to contact a friend at the FBI about public library reading lists. As a result, they get the lead to John Doe's (Kevin Spacey) apartment—the turning point into the second half of the film. This midpoint is dramatized with the confrontation between John Doe and Mills. The second half of act two starts with Somerset and Mills getting into John Doe's apartment, trying to figure out who their man is. This shifts the action from the first to the second half of the film. In the first half the detectives don't know who their man is; in the second half they do. But as the second half develops, their problem is that even though they have a name and an address, the name is meaningless and John Doe is still at large committing crimes.

In *American Beauty*, the first part of act two shows Lester's response to overhearing Angela's remarks about him. He starts pumping iron, smoking pot, and speaking out, not only at work but also at home to Carolyn. She doesn't know how to react. Instead of dealing with him, she starts an affair with Buddy. Lester quits his job and blackmails his boss into a nifty severance package and then, in some crazy attempt at regaining his youth, takes a job at the local fast-food restaurant. Lost in the middle of this confusion is Jane. With Angela making sexual comments about her dad, Jane finds solace in a tentative relationship with Ricky, also from a dysfunctional family and willing to kill her dad (information the audience gets at the opening of the film). The midpoint climaxes with Carolyn reacting to the news that Lester quit his job and confronting him about it through Jane, forcing him to tell her, which he does with gusto and asparagus. The family is splitting apart.

The second half of a film's second act focuses on the second act climax. New developments give way to rising conflict based on the actions already established. There are still surprises, but all are predicated on what we've learned in the first half of the film.

In *Se7en*, the detectives are inside John Doe's apartment. They seem to have found their man, or at least hope they'll get a lead on who he is. But all comes to naught when the evidence in his apartment doesn't get them any nearer to identifying and stopping him. Still at large, John Doe commits more heinous acts. Somerset starts to crack but continues to press his worldview on Mills, who rejects it and forces the older man into a corner. Near the end of act two, Somerset can't live with this attitude any longer—he breaks and tells Mills he will stay on and help him as long as there are any leads to follow. He has made a significant change from the beginning of act one to the end of act two. Then, on the heels of this action, with two of the Seven Deadly Sins left to discover, John Doe turns himself in; at the climax of act two, they have their man.

In *American Beauty*, the second half of act two starts with Carolyn's response to Lester's transformation; she begins to change as well. Her affair and shooting at the range empower her, but not enough to deal with the new Lester. Jane arranges for Angela to spend the night and confronts her father over his behavior toward her. Lester lashes out at Jane, immediately regretting it, but it's too late. The tension rises at home, as well as at Ricky's house, where Ricky's father, Colonel Fitts (Chris Cooper), grows suspicious of his son's involvement with Lester and finds the boy's videos. Carolyn and Buddy then make the mistake of driving through Mr. Smiley's, the fast-food restaurant where Lester works. He realizes she's been having an affair and states, "You don't get to tell me what to do. Ever again." This climaxes the second act. The marriage is over.

Act Three

Act three focuses on resolving the conflict. It grows out of the resulting situation at the end of act two, building the action with the final developments leading us to the peak point at the act three climax. At the end of act two in *Se7en*, John Doe has turned himself in. Now Somerset and Mills have their man; he's off the street. But there's a complication: Doe says there are two more crimes, and unless they consent to his conditions, he won't reveal where the bodies are. The detectives take the bait and agree. They prepare, taking no chances with him, but still feel uneasy. John Doe guides them to the last crime scene, where the opposing forces explode in the final crisis and climax that shows the outcome of this conflict and determines the final meaning of the film.

Act three of *American Beauty* develops similarly, but as a drama is less dependent on using the specific genre considerations of *Se7en*—i.e., resolving the crime. At the end of act two, Lester finds himself emancipated from the pretense of his marriage. But Carolyn suffers the repercussions; Buddy ends their affair. Ricky's father, already suspicious of Lester, misconstrues his son's drug deal for a sexual encounter. And when Angela arrives, coming onto Lester, his newfound security unnerves her and she retreats to Jane's bedroom. All of this serves as the basis of the conflict for the final crises of the act, which will detonate into the act three climax. The action ignites with Colonel Fitts busting Ricky and kicking him out, then coming onto Lester who compassionately rejects him. Jane all but begs Angela not to have sex with her dad, but Angela eggs Jane on until Ricky arrives to ask Jane to leave with him. When Angela ridicules their plan, Ricky responds with brutal honesty that sends her retreating in tears. Carolyn, crying in her car, refuses "to be a victim" and produces her gun from her glove compartment before heading home. None of this bodes well for Lester, who discovers Angela alone and vulnerable.

Now we're into the climax; is he going to get what he's wanted since the night of the basketball game? The climax builds tension through intercutting (Lester and Angela in the living room move closer to sex; Jane and Ricky in her bedroom plan their getaway; Carolyn drives home with a gun) coupled with the audience's prior knowledge that Lester will die. Then, at the climax, Lester learns that Angela's a virgin. His humanity emerges, and instead of sleeping with her, he comforts the confused girl. As the rest unfolds, almost feeling anticlimactic, Lester asks Angela the question he asked his daughter near the beginning of the movie: How is Jane? Angela makes a face and answers, "She thinks she's in love," and her answer makes him smile with gratitude. Angela leaves and as Lester reflects on this wonderful news, he's murdered. His death almost feels like the resolution to the movie, answering the question of who killed him and allowing the full meaning of the story to be expressed through his narration.

If you look at these basic plot summaries, the cause-and-effect relationships between the main focal points of the stories—the opening, inciting incident, act one climax, midpoint, act two climax, and act three climax—should be apparent: Actions lead to reactions, which create new actions, and so on. You can see the effect the conflict has on the characters in a progression of emotion and character transformation. These become the movements of the acts, constructed of scene relationships that carry the story forward and ensure that the audience follows along. Inside these act movements, we find groups of scenes working together to create meaning and momentum. These scene groups can be thought of as the *segments* or chapters of your story.

FILM SEGMENTS

There are between seven and thirteen story segments that make up a feature film, depending on its length. Each segment has a specific focus, objective, or theme. It dramatizes a section of the story with definite cause-and-effect scene plotting and generally moves the characters in one direction or another with regard to the overall plot goal, an individual objective, and/or the theme of the film. This strengthens the causal relationships between the scenes and builds a film's momentum. It helps the audience stay focused on the action, pushing the plot ahead even as the story tracks the characters' emotions, motivations, and reactions to what they encounter in the story.

The first act is usually made up of two or three segments, building from opening through the inciting incident to the act one climax, although there may be four segments if the act is long. Act two becomes more complex. The first half of act two is often made up of two to four segments building to the midpoint; and the second half usually contains the same. Act three might have one, two, or three segments that lead to the climax and resolution. It all depends on the film.

A film segment is similar to a chapter in a book. It covers an aspect of the story, building from a beginning point through the development of the problems/conflict, to culminate a section of the story, and then moves us into the next. *Master and Commander*, not a great movie but a highly watchable one, succeeds on the basis of how each well-developed segment leads into the next. Look carefully and you can see clearly where each episode begins, how it builds and finally climaxes, leaving a specific aspect of the story fully dramatized. The film's first segment is a chase that ends in disaster. The next section is about repairing the ship, and so on.

Below are examples of how the segments might break down in *Se7en* and *American Beauty.*

Segment Breakdown: Se7en

SEGMENT	TITLE	TIME
Act One		
Segment 1.	Somerset	Opening–0:07:00
Segment 2.	The Crime	0:08:00–0:17:00
Segment 3.	The Connection	0:17:08–0:29:30
Act Two		
Segment 4.	Coming Together	0:30:00–0:40:50
Segment 5.	The Red Herring	0:41:00–0:54:00
Segment 6.	Mills's World	0:54:00–1:01:40
Segment 7.	The Break! **(Midpoint)**	1:01:45–1:14:00
Segment 8.	Into the Killer's World	1:14:00–1:22:45
Segment 9.	Rock Bottom	1:23:00–1:33:00
Segment 10.	The Surrender	1:34:00–1:39:00
Act Three		
Segment 11.	The Trap	1:40:00–2:01:00

The titles of each segment indicate the main idea around which the sequence develops. Other information may be cut in, but these main ideas provide the focus for each segment. The titles also suggest the story's progression. We can clearly see the connections and development in the progression. Notice, too, that *Se7en*'s midpoint doesn't come exactly halfway through the film, but the segment leading up to it starts there. All of this helps keep a story moving, the main ideas focused, and the audience paying attention.

Segment Breakdown: American Beauty

SEGMENT	TITLE	TIME
Act One		
Segment 1.	Dead Already	Opening–0:13:00
Segment 2.	Waking Up	0:14:00–0:20:00
Segment 3.	Ricky's World	0:20:15–0:29:30
Segment 4.	Breaking Out	0:30:00–0:39:00
Act Two		
Segment 5.	Surprises	0:40:00–0:50:45
Segment 6.	Nothing to Lose **(Midpoint)**	0:51:00–1:07:30
Segment 7.	What Happened to Us?	1:07:45–1:17:00
Segment 8.	Truth or Lies	1:17:50–1:28:45
Act Three		
Segment 9.	The Reality of False Impressions	1:29:00–1:41:00
Segment 10.	I Want You	1:42:00–1:49:00
Segment 11.	All the Beauty	1:49:00–1:55:45

In *American Beauty*, we see a fuller first act than in *Se7en* because it has more characters to establish. As with *Se7en*, the titles suggest a progression in the story, and the point each segment is making. But unlike *Se7en*, it's not constrained by the specific genre requirements—the plot problem of murder. Its concern is the dramatic revelation of ordinary life. This isn't to say it's a better movie. *Se7en*, like *Chinatown*, takes the genre into the realm of American tragedy. But they are still essentially bound by the murders. Although *American Beauty* sets up a murder, it is not the central element of the story.

Audiences understand stories in terms of cause-and-effect events: This happened and so that happened. Segments lead your audience from one important point to the next. They build momentum because they show the relationship between what happened, why, and what resulted in the connecting scenes. They add emotional power by making a story point an emotional point when they include the emotional reactions a character has to a particular problem or event. And they help the audience better follow along by keeping the cause-and-effect relationships clear.

Scene and Action Sequences

Within a story segment you will often find smaller sequences of scenes, linked together through actions and reactions around a specific mini-storyline. Hollywood calls these *action* or *scene sequences*. They have a beginning, middle, and an end that set up a situation, develop it through conflict, and end at a climax, all without interruption from another plot element or subplot. Scene sequences play a major role in the construction of film segments because they keep the plot focused on the plot action as the characters work to achieve their goals.

Action sequences utilize obstacles and crises, and so they build tension. In action sequences, the obstacles generally present a direct threat to the protagonist and his immediate goals. This gives the hero something specific he's trying to accomplish, and the obstacles are there to prevent him from doing just that. These sequences use physical action, peril, and violent confrontation. The choreography of the action is clear cause and effect, where we are dramatizing a specific action and confrontation, which builds to a climax and resolution of this particular beat. Car chases, shootouts, or any other daring feats in action movies are clear examples.

Scene sequences are similar to action sequences but don't as a rule involve violent confrontation. They generally do not put the protagonist in direct conflict with the antagonist. But there is still a problem that must be faced. The scenes are structured in cause-and-effect relationships that show the protagonist of the sequence trying to accomplish something. Scenes are structured around the character meeting an obstacle, complication, or problem and then showing how he deals with it. The final ten minutes of *Se7en*, with the men riding out to the last crime scene, is a scene sequence. The basketball game where Lester's fantasy engages in *American Beauty* is another.

Sometimes a sequence will make up an entire segment, as in Segment 5 of *Se7en*, "The Red Herring." This action sequence starts with the captain (R. Lee Ermey) telling the detectives, "We have a winner." The lab has matched fingerprints to a name. Armed with an address, SWAT mobilizes, with the detectives in tow. The action follows their preparation, as well as the development as they locate building and then proceed to stalk their perpetrator, climaxing in the discovery of the latest victim. That third act of *Witness* is one long action sequence showing the confrontation between Book and the bad cops.

But often the sequences are smaller and contribute to the momentum of the larger segment. The opening segment of *American Beauty*, "Dead Already," establishes the family. After the opening video of Jane talking about murdering her father, Lester narrates a series of scenes setting up the Burnhams' world. About ten minutes into the movie, Carolyn arrives at her open house. The home is a dump and she must clean it, but it makes no difference. By the end of the day, she's been beaten down and even insulted by potential buyers. She responds with an emotional outburst that climaxes the sequence when she must hit herself to calm down. This ends the opening segment introducing all of the main characters except Angela.

Scene sequences enlarge the scope of the main conflict as well as contribute to a film's momentum and suspense by actively playing out how the characters deal with problems. The end of a scene sequence sometimes leads to the character taking new actions, though not in every case. Often scene sequences serve to complete an entertaining section of the plot that helps the audience empathize with the character.

CHAPTER 7

THE REAL ART OF PLOTTING

For many people plot is the same thing as structure. Both deal with designing the story, creating relationships between its elements and developing how action builds to a climax. When you structure a film story, you're working out the plot to discover the best way of telling it.

Real structure gives you the organizing principles for your material. It is far more than plot points, turning points, act breaks, or whatever you choose to call them. Structure gives you a framework to manage and make sense of all your material—the action, conflict, characters, exposition, theme, subtext, etc. It creates the context for this complex interplay of elements. Yet in the finest films, structure is treated with an underlying simplicity that is as elegant and graceful as quantum physics.

Plotting, on the other hand, is the nuts and bolts of putting your material together. The neat and tidy architect of structure becomes the plot contractor and craftsman who get calluses and broken nails along with all the ensuing problems of turning the plan into the project.

Plotting turns the structural story considerations that have to do with conflict and meaning into moments that convey exposition, build suspense, reveal character, and expose emotion. All of this deepens the audience's involvement in the work. It is the art of creating the relationships between your scenes to make your story points more powerful and meaningful.

Writing a screenplay is a multifaceted process. First you need an overall plan that gives shape and meaning to the material. The next step is the actual outlining or plotting of the scenes to create the path of action and reaction that builds tension, meaning, and emotion. The last step is writing the scenes that accomplish this.

The real art of plotting is affecting a naturalness in your storytelling, creating an aesthetic flow of the material so that your audience never has the need or time to question or criticize the sequence of events shown. It all has to come together for them the way you want them to experience it. It's not just a record of events. That's what docudrama is for. F. Scott Fitzgerald noted over seventy years ago that, in screenwriting, scenes need to be carefully written and ordered in such a way that the audience has no choice but to feel exactly the way the filmmaker wants them to feel. Whether it's your screenplay or film, you want the audience to experience the events of the story so they come to your conclusion.

What follows now are ideas to help you achieve this: the real art of plotting.

TRANSFORMING PLOT POINTS INTO PLOTTED POINTS

In so many scripts, writers fail to understand the full dimension and power of their midpoint and act climaxes. Syd Field calls these plot points, Linda Seger refers to them as turning points; whatever you name them they are the climaxes of the major movements of the story. Writers may come up with dramatic incidents that should promise significant change and development in their scripts, but the ways these events are played often leave readers flat. The impact is lost because writers don't know how to use the information effectively—i.e., dramatically. The incidents become just one more scene in the chain of scenes of a story.

These climaxes are the most significant moments in your story—your plot hinges on them. They need time to develop. They don't just appear as a scene and disappear. The most memorable climaxes are emotional as well as action packed. Something important happens that drives the story to its next phase and into a higher gear. It has a dramatic effect that will cause a change in the plot as a result of your protagonist's actions and/or reactions. An outline may put this idea in one scene. But if it's one scene, it had better be a damn good one—a fantastic one—to move your characters and your audience.

Great movies pay special attention to these moments. The act breaks take time—meaning often more than one scene—to develop. This group of scenes makes up a sequence and generally needs exposition to set up the action leading to the climax, the significant action, and then shows the dramatic result. The goal here isn't to simply write a plot point. You must plot an action that builds to the important climax and show the reaction that will 1) change the direction of the plot, 2) change the audience's understanding of what's happening, and 3) up the stakes of the story. This means you want your audience to experience the action, not just understand it.

You can help the audience get into the flow of the action by setting up the event. This gives them a better understanding of what's happening and adds more significance to the action because you're weighting it with more screen time. Because this is important action, leading to a change in the story, there is usually a dramatic effect on the characters. This is shown in their emotional responses, marking the event as either a good turn in the action or a bad one. When the characters, especially the protagonist, don't react to the dramatic consequences, the audience won't react either. We have to know the event is important, and the character's strong emotional response tells us.

The end of the first act of *Catch Me If You Can* shows Frank (Leonardo DiCaprio) running away from home. But look how the idea develops, in the course of several scenes. The setup of the sequence starts on the street, with Frank walking home from school. He notes a strange car parked out in front of his building, not unlike one he saw a few scenes earlier. That car turned out to belong to his father's friend, Jack Barnes (James Brolin), who was discreetly visiting with his mother. Suspicious, Frank enters his home and finds a man's jacket tossed over a chair. He grabs it and starts going through the pockets when the man emerges from a back room, startling him. Frank yells at him to get out of there, but the man turns out to be an attorney, and he asks Frank to come with him. "We've all been waiting for you," he says.

To his surprise, and the audience's, Frank's parents are in here, with the attorney, making arrangements for their divorce. His mother tries to talk to him, but he's in shock. They want Frank to choose whom he'll live with—his mother or father. The attorney instructs the shaken kid to go in the next room and write down a name on the court papers. But Frank can't. The next scene shows him running down the street, away from his problem. He runs until he arrives at the train station where he asks for a ticket, proceeding to pay for it with a check.

This climaxes the first section of the story, showing the events that put the young Frank Abagnale on the road to becoming a con artist. The sequence takes five minutes to play out. The plot action is now focused on the problem of his survival, a kid in the real world on his own, and how he starts scheming to survive.

The end of the first act of *Shakespeare in Love* brings Will and Viola together. They experience love at first sight, which results in Will's breaking through his writer's block. But the climax must be set up. It starts with Will chasing after Viola, who is impersonating Thomas Kent and has just auditioned for a part in Will's new but unwritten play. Will pursues Viola as Thomas to the De Lessepses' home, where we learn she's to be married to Lord Wessex (Colin Firth) in two week's time. Will arrives with a note for Thomas Kent, which the Nurse takes for Viola. He waits around for a response. When none comes, he heads out but meets musicians arriving for a party. Wessex arrives, too. As a playwright always up for free food and entertainment, Will goes in with the band. Wessex arranges his marriage with Viola's father, while Viola plays the dutiful daughter, making her rounds at the party when Will sees her. He can't take his eyes off her. When they connect, it's clear she feels the same way. Before things heat up too much, Wessex whisks Will away and threatens his life. But Will waits around and discovers Viola pining for him on her balcony. He announces himself, and it's clear how she feels about him. Although he's thwarted in his attempt to steal a kiss, he returns to his room and writes—his writer's block gone!

The setup builds on the sequence that precedes it, leading us to the moment when the two lovers inevitably meet as man and woman. The chemistry that heats up Will's and Viola's hearts as they dance together touches our hearts, too. We know from previous scenes how she feels about him and experience their longing with them.

The point of this section is to get the lovers together so Will can break through his creative block. This turns the story in a new direction. During act one, Will has been blocked creatively; first because the woman in his life is another man's mistress and then because he discovers she has yet another master on the side. Will is at the mercy of his muse, and as long as she loves him he can write, but once betrayed he can't get a word on paper. Meeting Viola he is again ripe with rhyme and inspiration. And even though the situation poses great danger, he must pursue it for all that it offers him creatively. At the end of act one he is writing furiously. This moves us into the next section of the plot: He's creating the play that Viola will star in as his alter ego, Romeo, thus keeping them close until the next development in the love story occurs. This sequence lasts almost twelve minutes.

Both these examples create strong lines of action that develop tension and meaning. They set up the action of the plot so that we understand the problem/conflict/action the protagonist confronts at the start of the sequence: Frank is worried about his mother's faltering affections for his father; Will is trying to find Thomas Kent for his play. They develop through conflict, turning the plot line in a new direction: Frank leaves home with twenty-five dollars in his bank account; Will finds a new muse and starts writing again. We also see the stakes for the characters increase: Frank is just a kid going out into the world on his own; Viola is promised to Wessex and he has promised to kill Will.

A good climax, whether it comes at the end of the first, second, or third acts, or at the midpoint, is also surprising. Whatever the result is, if your audience anticipates the event, especially at the conclusion of the plot, they will find it unsatisfying. You want to remember to plot these points out with conflict. Conflict threatens your character's success and leads the audience to doubt the outcome. It also focuses your audience on the immediate problem at hand, so that they are less likely to see your true intention.

Both our examples surprise us. In *Catch Me If You Can*, no one is expecting Frank to walk in on his parents, working out divorce issues. Similarly, no one would imagine the lines in *Shakespeare in*

Love to come straight out of *Romeo and Juliet*.

Although we don't want the final climax to be predictable, it must still feel inevitable. It is the end result of all the action; the forces coming together in a final clash, giving us a result that proves the story's premise. Everything has been leading to this moment. The audience has to feel that, given everything that's happened in the plot up to this point, it's the only way the story could have turned out. It's fate.

Remember, too, that how the film turns out in the end must be appropriate to the characters, the conflict, the theme, and the genre. If characters take actions that are contrary to the personalities you've set up, it won't feel right. You must have incorporated the reasons *why* in the plot of the story. If its genre is a romantic comedy, it has to end with romance and comedy, not tragedy and death. If it's an action movie, the audience probably expects action at the finale; ending in a boardroom is not going to cut it.

DEEPENING OUR CHARACTERIZATIONS ALONG WITH AUDIENCE INVOLVEMENT

Many writers spend a lot of time building a solid act structure and plotting the turning points for their stories but don't really consider how the audience will connect with their characters. They focus on the action and think this will be strong enough to capture the audience's interest. If they consider their characters, they create them with complicated back stories or a bevy of idiosyncrasies, but as we've seen in previous chapters, it's what characters do, especially in the face of conflict, that really shows us who they are.

When we create drama, we're focusing on dramatic events that result from characters in conflict. The audience's perceptions of the characters grow out of what they learn about these people from their actions, reactions, choices, and decisions in the face of their difficulties. When we're trying to create characterizations our audience can relate to, feel for, and become involved with, the key is getting to the emotion and using it. Remember, it's more important for your audience to "get" your character emotionally than to have a complete intellectual understanding of the psychological explanations for a character's actions; it's harder to relate to cerebral reasons than to emotional ones.

The goal is to use the characters' emotions in ways that keep the action moving and still represent the core of who they are. The really great writers create actions motivated in the characters' emotional reactions that demonstrate who these characters are. In *Erin Brockovich*, Erin is fired from Ed's law office at the end of act one. Oblivious to why, she returns home frustrated, angry, and confused. What does she find? A mess in her kitchen and George under the sink. She scolds him for being there, and then a cockroach scampers out from under his tools. She freaks, cursing, stamping at it, and screams at the top of her lungs, "Who lives like this? What kind of person lets her kids run around in a house crawling with bugs the size of house cats?" In this one moment, we feel her pain as she blames herself for her condition. The writer has created a situation in which Erin can first take out her anger on George for being there, but then, with the invention of the cockroach and the outburst that follows, show us the true source of her distress: anger at herself. In the two scenes that follow, Erin's vulnerability develops, and she opens up enough to let George in, and us with him.

At the midpoint of *One Flew Over the Cuckoo's Nest*, McMurphy (Jack Nicholson) finally realizes he's not serving out his jail time in the mental hospital; the doctors and nurses will decide when he gets out based on his behavior. He asks Nurse Ratched (Louise Fletcher) about it in group therapy. The result is the further revelation that almost all of the patients on the ward have voluntarily committed themselves. McMurphy can't believe it and admonishes them to get out of there, saying they're "no more crazy" than anybody else out on the street. This serves to subtly motivate the other patients to stand up to Ratched.

Cheswick (Sydney Lassick) decides to confront Nurse Ratched about her rationing the patients' cigarettes because of McMurphy's poker playing. She tries to settle him down with her usual condescension, but Cheswick feels empowered. He works himself up into a tantrum, just as some childish silliness between the patients involving Harding (William Redfield) and his cigarettes suddenly explodes. In the middle of this, a frenzied Cheswick screams, "I ain't no little kid, Nurse Ratched, I ain't no little kid," as poor McMurphy looks on, shocked and confused. With no one paying any attention to the aggrieved Cheswick, McMurphy charges over to the nurses' station, breaks the glass, and grabs a cigarette carton. He offers the cigarettes to Cheswick, who is inconsolable. The attendant, Washington (Nathan George), has begun to cart Cheswick off. This provokes McMurphy, and he tries to stop Washington only to have the attendant turn his rage on him. The confrontation escalates, and by the end of the scene McMurphy, Cheswick, and the Chief are all on their way for electroshock treatment.

The key action here is McMurphy breaking the windowpane to get Cheswick his cigarettes. Through this action, the writers show that McMurphy feels something for Cheswick and is trying to help him, even if it's the wrong way. This is one of the reasons the audience feels so much for McMurphy: He cares for the other patients in the asylum, as demonstrated through his actions.

Near the beginning of *American Beauty*, we go with Carolyn to her open house. "I will sell this house today," is her mantra as she cleans and scrubs, getting the home ready for potential buyers. But the day goes horribly, and after a particularly bad encounter with a couple, she breaks. As her tears spill, we're shocked to see her slap herself repeatedly until she stops crying. After a few deep breaths, she has everything under control. She pulls the blinds and leaves, all business. But we have been afforded a glimpse of the deep despair with which Carolyn lives.

Successful movies are filled with these scenes. Remember when Peter Parker (Toby Maguire) discovers his powers in the first *Spider-Man*? His screams of joy as he sails over the rooftops make us smile with his delight. Or think of the sequence in *Groundhog Day* when Phil (Bill Murray) has lost all hope. Each day he tries to kill himself, climaxing in his kidnapping of the groundhog, driving to the quarry, and crashing his car over the edge. His actions show us just how desperate he really is.

Or think of the scene in *Jaws*, when Quint and Hooper (Richard Dreyfuss) compare scars on the *Orca*, each trying to "out-macho" the other. Their competitive kidding provides the humorous lead-in to one of the more memorable scenes in the movie: when Quint tells the story of the USS *Indianapolis* and clues us in to his deep hatred of sharks. The point of the scene is to give us the exposition about the USS *Indianapolis*, but the end result is to humanize the characters and bring them closer to the audience.

PLOTTING FOR EMOTION AND NOT SENTIMENTALITY

This brings us to another aspect of emotion: sentimentality. Over and over I hear students tell me the reason they don't include any emotional reactions in their scripts is that they fear being sentimental. My answer is this: Since when is real emotion sentimentality? Sentimentality is superficial emotion; one reacts viscerally but lacks true depth of feeling. Real emotion is what connects us. It makes a story real. And if it's not on the page, or only vaguely implied, your readers are not going to get it, and that means they're less likely to connect with your script.

Great movies contain scenes that create an emotional context for the characters and story. These scenes (or beats of scenes) trigger empathy and identification within the audience, leading them to engage with the story on a deeper level. Great filmmakers find and use these moments. Sometimes the emotion is the whole point of the scene; sometimes these emotions are tied to actions that make the emotion all the more significant; and sometimes the emotion is contained within a reaction.

In *Erin Brockovich*, there is a scene late in act two that begins by showing the audience the PG&E plant, late at night. Then hands gather up stones. The hands belong to Jensen (Michael Harney), Donna's (Marg Helgenberger) husband, and he stands facing the plant. Suddenly, he hurls a rock at the plant, and then another, and another, screaming his pain soundlessly. The rocks fall far short of their target. Finally, he sinks to his knees and breaks down, and the audience feels his pain.

The next scene starts with Erin sitting on the edge of Donna's bed, listening, while Donna reveals she's just been diagnosed with a malignant tumor. Jensen stands in the background, never uttering a word. Now the audience understands Jensen's action a scene back and empathizes with him. It brings the audience closer to the characters and more deeply into the story.

If you show your character sad and crying over every disappointment, or giddy and high over every success, your script will become tiresome and off-putting. Instead, you want to play those moments of emotion that are the most dramatically productive; the ones that help the audience connect to and deepen their understanding of the characters. These beats will usually come close to the more significant and life-changing parts of the plot. Obviously, this means the act breaks. But, as illustrated above, emotion is necessary where important actions and events demand a response.

You want to dig deeply into the characters' emotional lives to discover what they truly feel. Then you need to find a way to communicate creatively that emotion to the audience, to coax them into a state of empathy. This will help the audience understand the characters' motivations, and the potential cost of their actions.

These moments can be big or small. The right reaction given at the end of a scene, the smallest touch, can have a profound effect on the audience. The 1946 Academy Award–winning *The Best Years of Our Lives* is loaded with scenes that make the audience feel and connect with the characters, because of the use of real emotion. Near the beginning, when the three men arrive home after the end of WWII, one each from the infantry (Al [Fredric March]), air corps (Fred [Dana Andrews]), and navy (Homer [Harold Russell]), they share a cab ride into Boone City. Homer, who's lost both his hands, is dropped off first. Al and Fred watch, with us, from the cab as his family rushes out onto the lawn to greet him. His mother sees his prosthetic hooks, gasps in anguish, and then catches herself. His fiancée (Cathy O'Donnell) hugs him, but Homer's arms remain rigid at his sides. She moves back, and then there is just silence. Heartbreaking, gut-wrenching silence. It's hard not to feel the pain. Just when the tension seems almost unbearable, Homer's little sister runs out of the house and flies to him, excited and happy. The point of the scene is to get Homer home and show the effect of his disability on his family and then how this affects him. Through the simple but honest reactions of all the characters involved in this one significant moment, we are drawn deeply into their lives and the story.

Once you've found the emotion and come up with a creative way to get it across, the final thing to remember is this: *Don't rush it.* Real feeling needs time to play out so that the audience can experience and process it. When you have the emotion, play it for real, and see where it takes you in the scene.

I'm reminded of another scene from *The Best Years of Our Lives*, when Fred, the former captain and bombardier, can't get anything to go right for him. He decides to leave town and goes to the airport to hitch a ride east or west, whichever plane can take him first. He has to wait for a flight, so he goes for a walk. He finds acres and acres of used-up warplanes, bombers, fighters, and cargo planes, all ready for the junk heap. In an earlier scene we've seen that he's haunted by his war experiences, but now he walks and walks, until he finally climbs up into a bomber and gets into the turret. The soundtrack in the film mimics engines turning on and sputtering to life. In the script are voices of men, calling out for help as a problem arises, but in the film we hear none of them. The focus is all on Fred, as he sits there, shaken, reliving probably the worst moments of his life. And we feel it. The moment is all about understanding him. The scene ends when a foreman calls out to Fred, and after some initial disagreement, winds up offering him a job.

PREPARATIONS AND CONSEQUENCES

The true emotions characters display enhance the audience's experience of a story. Emotion brings the audience closer to the material, makes them more available to the storyteller, and ultimately deepens their understanding of what it's all about. But if screenwriters get carried away with emotion, they're apt to sacrifice the plot's momentum. Even as we look for ways to strengthen the audience's emotional connection to our stories, we can't lose sight of the rising action that must build through obstacles and complications, to crisis, climax, and resolution.

One way to heighten our audience's involvement with the characters as well as keep them focused on the story's forward progression is to build a plot line that incorporates both event and emotion. Cause-and-effect plotting emphasizes action and reaction to create sequences that move the action forward and show the emotional effect on the characters. When a writer constructs a sequence based on the idea of *preparations and consequences*, he uses cause-and-effect plotting to bring emotion out of the characters, which in turn affects the audience and keeps the plot action moving ahead.

The idea behind preparations and consequences is simple enough: You show the protagonist or another major character preparing for the dramatic event, then after the event plays out, you show the audience the result. Both the preparation for something important and its consequence offer the screenwriter the opportunity to include emotional content while building momentum through a sequence of scenes that uses directed action: action directed at a specific outcome. This keeps the story moving forward while the audience still gets to connect with the characters. The focus on the lead-in to the conflict scenes as well as on the outcome of the event adds dramatic weight to the action and makes the event more memorable. These scenes allow the audience time to worry about the future of the characters as they prepare, so that viewers and readers can feel with them in the aftermath.

A scene of preparation consists of an important character (or characters) getting ready for the approaching dramatic event. Sports movies and war films contain the most obvious examples of this type of setup. Think of *Friday Night Lights*, *Invincible*, or *Miracle*. All have locker room scenes in which coaches psyche up the athletes for the big game. The audience sees the young men serious and nervous and feels their tension with them. War films play the scenes before the battle to show us the soldiers bracing for it. Think of *Saving Private Ryan* and *The Thin Red Line*. Soldiers wait, and through their outward show of emotion (or lack of it) the audience feels the pressure and import of the impending action

105 BUFFALO WAY-P.O. BOX
JACKSON, WY 83001
Phone # (307) 733-5950
Store Director - Michael Edwards
Cashier: Denise H

02/12/12 15:53:09

PREFERRED CUSTOMER: XXXXXXX1695

GROCERY

WRGLY ORBIT GUM PC 2200000488	1.25	F
=> 1.00 AFTER PREFERRED SAVINGS	-.25	F

HOME HEALTH BEAUTY

EQUAL ASPIRIN PC 4116343223	5.99	T
EQUAL ASPIRIN PC 4116343223	5.99	T
=> FREE ITEM	-5.99	T
SNDWN VITAMINS 3076848880	8.99	
CHAPSTICK 3057315915	3.09	T
SUBTOTAL	19.07	
TAX 1	.54	
TOTAL	19.61	
Visa TENDER	19.61	

Acct: XXXXXXXXXXXX0933
APPRVL CODE 00152D
Cas Ref# 21334
Cash CHANGE .00

NUMBER OF ITEMS 5

*********** SAVINGS SUMMARY ***********

PREFERRED SAVINGS

****

TODAY'S TOTAL SAVINGS 6.28
THAT IS A SAVINGS OF 25%

****

Trx:121 Oper:119 Term: 6 Store: 183
02/12/12 15:53:39

Thank You For Shopping At
ALBERTSONS

Pharmacy Phone # (307) 733-9223

www.albertsons.com

Customer Questions
or Party Tray Orders
1-877-932-7948

****

Enter to be a weekly winner
of a $100 gift card!!
Go to: www.albertsonslistens.com
Enter Code: 02120 18330 060121
Take the survey within 3 days0271eA

****

with them. Tension builds for the audience during these scenes because they feel the characters' anxiety and worry about the potential outcomes. If the event isn't truly important, however, at least to the character, his anxieties, excitement, or anticipation will feel forced and undercut exactly what you're trying to achieve.

Most films make use of preparation scenes somewhere in their plots. Several times, *Se7en* readies the audience along with the characters for upcoming events. Once the detectives have the lead to the "Sloth" crime scene, a big buildup illustrates the SWAT team getting ready to move on the location. A lot of time is spent showing policemen being briefed and readied before they shove off. In act three, we see Somerset and Mills preparing to go with John Doe to the last crime scene. It starts with the men in the washroom shaving their chests for the wires they'll be wearing. Somerset does his best to prepare Mills, wanting him to be ready for anything. If the man in the moon should pop out of his head, "I want you to expect it," he says. Then Mills makes a small joke and the two men laugh, the audience with them. But as they return to their work, the seriousness of the situation overtakes them, and words slip away. They're worried; the audience sees it in their faces and their reactions. The next shot shows the men in silence, buttoning their shirts over their wires, putting on bulletproof vests and their holsters. Then they check their guns. All of this communicates to the audience the life-or-death nature of the situation they face. We then cut to John Doe, in orange jumpsuit, head shaved, hands cuffed, escorted down the stairs. The sequence builds until all three are in the car, helicopters flying over them, other vehicles monitoring their every move; all the while the looming catastrophe hangs in the future.

The interesting thing about this sequence is that it readies the audience for another scene that is still meant to prepare them for the climax. John Doe, Mills, and Somerset get into the car on their way to the real dramatic event, the final revelation of the crimes. All of this heightens the tension by increasing the audience's worry. It plays into how screenwriters build suspense, which I'll talk about next.

Dramas and comedies use scenes of preparation and consequence, too. In *One Flew Over the Cuckoo's Nest*, after the ruckus over the cigarettes (spurred on by Mac's revelation), McMurphy, Cheswick, and the Chief are all carted off. The three men are led down a hallway and seated outside a room to wait. McMurphy doesn't know what's happening and is his usual lighthearted self, the Chief keeps up his mute, impassive facade, but clearly Cheswick knows what's coming. He whimpers while Mac watches, puzzled by his reaction. The attendants carry Cheswick into the room. McMurphy watches, clueless, but the audience can anticipate what's next: electroshock therapy. What's wonderfully original about this sequence is how the audience starts to worry about McMurphy before he does, through the use of Cheswick's character. As Mac and the Chief wait their turn, tension builds. Then Mac offers the Chief a stick of gum, and the real revelation comes: The Chief speaks. "Thanks," he says. Shocked, McMurphy offers him another stick just to be sure he heard right and is delighted to be in on the Chief's secret. And now, while the audience is still anticipating the upcoming treatment, they watch these men interact and plan their escape. This develops both men's characters and the audience's relationship with them. When the medical staff brings Cheswick out on a gurney, as still as death, the audience is feeling thick as thieves with Mac and the Chief, who see Cheswick, and quiet down. But McMurphy still doesn't get it. The attendants come for him, and, still tickled by the Chief's deception, he heads in with a spring in his step. In the room, he obliges the medical staff's every wish. With forehead swabbed, electrodes in place, mouthpiece between his teeth, they start and the audience sees the current hit him.

This sequence builds tension, using Cheswick's reactions as the barometer of events to come. As Mac and the Chief wait for Cheswick to finish his treatment, the audience anticipates the danger soon to befall the men. But then the writers disarm us. They let the two men connect and deepen the meaning of the story, adding another revelation to the sequence to make it an even stronger point in the plot of this Oscar-winning script.

The result of a dramatic event, shown in the consequences of the action or aftermath situation, puts the focus on what the action has cost or gained the characters, both physically and emotionally. We show the effect, and with it the emotional reaction to the success, failure, or draw. Here the characters process—try to make sense of—what's just happened, and the audience does the same. The time allows the situation to settle for the characters, as well as the audience, and it broadens our understanding of the events.

The consequence scene for the sequence above from *One Flew over the Cuckoo's Nest* starts back on the ward. The ubiquitous mood music is playing. The patients are sitting down for yet another therapy session with Nurse Ratched. It seems like an ordinary day. Then McMurphy enters, shambling dully across the room. The men's hearts sink—he's had a lobotomy. Even the Chief, who is in the back shuffling with his broom, looks dismayed. Then Mac suddenly jumps, scaring them, and he's back to his devil-may-care self, promising to be a good boy for Nurse Ratched and not cause any more trouble.

This scene works wonderfully. It offers a scare and then relieves with a laugh. It shows the audience that McMurphy is all right and that the result is that he now intends to behave himself knowing what the cost is if he doesn't.

Depending on the action, the consequence scene can be

dramatic or comedic. In the famous "Take no prisoners" scene from *Lawrence of Arabia*, Ali (Omar Sharif) walks through the carnage after the slaughter of the Turks, looking for Lawrence (Peter O'Toole). When he finally finds him, Lawrence is covered in blood from head to toe, shaking in horror as he drops his saber from his bloody hands. Ali walks away from him, now the more civilized man compared to the barbaric Lawrence.

Preparations and consequences often set the audience up for one result but then deliver its opposite. These are wonderful tools when plotting a reversal. The aftermath of the electroshock therapy scene for McMurphy is exactly this. The audience believes the worst has happened, but suddenly the scene spins and everything is all right. When the action completes in a surprising way, resulting not only in an unexpected turn of events but also a different emotional outcome, the audience experiences a stronger emotional impact.

The beginning of *Jerry Maguire* illustrates this beautifully. Jerry is laying out exposition for us, but he is really preparing his Mission Statement. His frantic intensity drives the action and reveals how important the Mission Statement—entitled "The Things We Think but Do Not Say, The Future of Our Business"—is to his psyche. Jerry has the memos copied and distributed. He returns to his hotel room, where he immediately has second thoughts. He tries to recall the memos, but it's too late. As he panics, the audience panics with him. Then in the following scene as he nervously prepares to enter the lobby the next day, he's met with applause. The audience is whipped around and smiling with him. As he exits the lobby, the focus shifts to two agents. "How long you give him?" asks the first agent. "Mmmm. A week," says the other. A second reversal hits the audience, and both feel right.

Preparations and consequences are strong tools for developing and outlining a plot. They'll help you design the sequence of scenes so that you know where you're placing the emotional emphasis. When actually writing these scenes, remember to find the emotion and use it in an interesting yet authentic way.

PLOTTING FOR SUSPENSE

All through this book I've talked about conflict and dramatic tension, which are the basis of *suspense*. People often use the words *tension* and *suspense* interchangeably, but they're not synonymous. *Tension* is the quality of being stretched tight, of being strained, anxious. Suspense creates this feeling. It triggers anxiety but also *the need to know what's going to happen next*. Suspense is based in the uncertainty the audience feels over the possible outcomes for the characters in difficult situations. They anticipate the trouble and still hope that everything will work out. The vacillation between these two poles increases pressure as well as the audience's need for a resolution.

Every movie, whether it's comedy, drama, action, or another genre, utilizes suspense in some way. Basic suspense in any story comes from the uncertainty we feel about the character caught in a specific conflict. The character has a goal, the conflict stands between her and it, and we speculate whether she'll succeed.

The key to getting basic suspense working starts with creating a real, substantial problem, one that is life threatening or life changing, for a protagonist the audience cares about. Generally, this is the main conflict of the film around which the other conflicts are plotted. It needs to have real consequences; should the protagonist fail something bad will happen, to her or to others. The secondary problems that demand the protagonist's attention can also be used to plot sequences as long as they pose a real threat to the character's success or well-being, thus also creating suspense.

In both *Se7en* and *American Beauty* suspense also emanates from the tension of relationships. In *Se7en*, the audience wants Somerset and Mills to reach a meeting of the minds and fear they won't. In *American Beauty*, the audience wants Lester to connect with his daughter in a meaningful way but worries he'll mess everything up by getting involved with her friend. Even in *Kill Bill, Vol. 2*, where Bill (David Carradine) has tried to kill Beatrix (Uma Thurman) time and again, when she finally discovers he's been living with their child at his villa, the audience still has the tiniest hope they will work out their differences while knowing that that kind of forgiveness would be hard even for Mother Teresa.

A real antagonist who is working against the protagonist also helps to create overall suspense within a plot. This means the antagonist has to be stronger and better equipped for the fight than the protagonist, someone who represents a real danger to your hero accomplishing his goal. This goes along with understanding the nature of your story's conflict and setting it up properly, as described in Chapter 3. Karen Eiffel in *Stranger than Fiction* is as strong an antagonist for Harold Crick as Darth Vader is for Luke Skywalker because they both represent tangible obstacles to each character's well-being.

As you plot out the individual scenes and sequences of your script, you're always looking for ways to create more tension and suspense, to keep the audience hooked. Here are a few ways.

Give the Audience Information

In Chapter 4, under "Foreshadowing Conflict" (see p. 61), I talked about showing the audience the trouble that lies ahead. This was the axiom of Alfred Hitchcock, the master of suspense. Hitchcock said that the essential factor in building real suspense is to give the audience more information than the protagonist and other characters have. This was key for him: Show the audience the danger looming that the characters don't see themselves, thereby placing the audience in a superior position. This creates tension, and the desire for the situation to resolve.

Hitchcock illustrated this point with the story of two men in a bar with a bomb under their table. If we viewers, along with the characters, don't know about the bomb, we wind up with a big surprise when it goes off, and that's it. However, if the audience knows about the bomb while the characters don't, and we know when it's set to go off, now we're in a suspenseful situation. As the minutes on the wall clock tick down, we're tense, engaged, and want to warn the characters to move. The audience is caught up in the moment-to-moment uncertainty of a situation that could go either way. We will sit through the most boring expository details with bated breath, waiting for the characters to discover the bomb or perish because they don't.

When plotting out a scene or a sequence, you want to consider if there's something threatening to your hero's success you can show to the audience before the character sees it. In Hitchcock's *North by Northwest*, the audience learns there is no George Kaplan long before Thornhill does and that the good spies have no intention of helping him escape the murder charges. Thornhill meets the lovely Eve Kendall (Eva Maria Saint) on the train, who helps him. We hope for the best. Then it's revealed to the audience she's in league with Vandamm (James Mason), the villain. Yikes! Tension ratchets up. When Thornhill leaves the train in Chicago, the station is crawling with cops. He disguises himself as a red cap and gets away, but not without the audience fearing he'll be caught. Hitchcock was a master of this. But so are other writers and directors.

In *The Fugitive*, the tension level rises every time Gerard and his agents figure out where Kimble is and show up in his vicinity before the good doctor knows he's been located. Sometimes we even see both characters in an area at the same time, without either one's knowledge of the other. This still creates suspense as we anticipate their meeting and the danger it poses for Kimble.

Most film stories encompass more than the hero's point of view, although often beginning writers stick only with the protagonist. A point of view that allows you to include other angles in the plot action will lead you to creating more suspenseful situations, and increasing audience involvement in the process. This is called *crosscutting*.

Crosscutting

In crosscutting we specifically intercut between the characters in conflict. The characters are on a collision course. Suspense builds as the two move closer to each other. Think of *The Fugitive* when Kimble is on that bus with the injured man and the train is getting closer and closer. He gets out, and the audience is relieved to see he's made it, until the train jumps the track and travels down into the ravine right after him.

Crosscutting is a staple of genre films, like action, horror, sci-fi, and thrillers. But comedies and dramas also use it. A wonderful sequence from the comedy *Diner* illustrates this nicely. In the second half of act two, things have gotten worse for Boogie (Mickey Rourke). He's been worked over by the loan shark's thugs, and now his latest bet about bedding Carol Heathrow (Colette Blonigan) has gone south with her catching the flu. It's over for him; the bookie's going to break his legs, if not kill him. Boogie suddenly sees salvation in taking out Shrevie's (Daniel Stern) unhappy and undervalued wife, Beth (Ellen Barkin), and dressing her up to pass her off as Carol. She doesn't know this and thinks she's having an evening with an old flame who cares about her.

Boogie picks her up and the two get in his car. He asks her to put on a wig so no one will know they're together. She is married, after all. When she puts on the wig that looks like Carol's hair, the audience knows for sure what Boogie intends. Now the film cuts to Shrevie and Fenwick (Kevin Bacon). Shrevie doesn't want to go home to his problems with Beth. He finds out Fenwick's going back to his apartment so he can validate Boogie's bet when he arrives with Carol. Shrevie thinks this sounds like fun—spying on his friend's seduction—and decides to tag along. Now the audience says "Uh-oh."

Back in the car, Boogie tells Beth that when they get to Fenwick's place, she can't say anything. She feels weird about this, but she is lonely and plays along. Cut back to Shrevie and Fenwick: They arrive at Fenwick's apartment and hide in his closet to wait. Cut back to Boogie and Beth, just long enough for the audience to feel that this isn't going to turn out well. Then, the film cuts back to the boys in the closet trying to make sure they get a good peek.

All the while the tension is escalating as the audience expects disaster to hit when the pairs meet. The car pulls up and Boogie and Beth get out. They enter the apartment lobby and head up the stairs. Shrevie and Fenwick try to keep quiet, waiting for Boogie to arrive with Carol. But he doesn't come. Back on the stairway, Boogie turns around and leads Beth outside. He can't go through with it. But throughout, the audience has felt terrible tension and suspense anticipating the catastrophe of Beth and Shrevie meeting.

Unexpected Complications

In a way, Shrevie joining Fenwick and the train careening off the track after Kimble are both *unexpected complications* that are plotted out to create maximum suspense. Unexpected complications are a great way to increase jeopardy and suspense, as well as tell us something about the character by their actions. These arise in many different forms, but the key here is focusing on the character who is trying to accomplish something important. The complication interferes with this and leads to more danger.

The Fugitive is loaded with these scenes. In one, Kimble has gotten himself back into Cook County Hospital, working as a janitor, hoping to find the one-armed man. He's been making progress when he finds himself in the middle of a crisis near ER. Dr. Eastman (Julianne Moore) corrals Kimble to help and take a patient, a young boy, to critical care. She hands over the boy's paperwork, but from the kid's symptoms, Kimble knows his condition is more serious than Dr. Eastman thinks. He wheels the boy off, reassuring the kid and checking the X-rays, while Dr. Eastman watches him. Once around the corner though, Kimble gets in the elevator and changes the orders, taking the boy directly to surgery and thus saving his life. The cost, however, is Kimble's exposure in the hospital. A few scenes later, Dr. Eastman confronts him over his action and then goes to report him. Kimble takes off, and now he can no longer move freely around the hospital in his quest for the one-armed man. But he willingly puts himself in harm's way, and through his action to save the boy's life we know what kind of a man he is.

Another technique of Hitchcock's was to have two things happen at once. The audience is focused on one action when another action interrupts it. This new action can be serious or humorous, but it's there only to get in the way. In *The Man Who Knew Too Much*, Dr. McKenna (James Stewart) and his wife, Jo (Doris Day), are in the middle of a tense phone call with their son's kidnappers when old friends of Jo's gaily arrive. The McKennas don't want to arouse suspicion, but need to focus. The audience feels the pressure with them as McKenna tries to be casual and amiable but can't hide his discomfort.

The Ticking Clock

Time is running out for the characters before the danger hits. I've already illustrated this with the example of the bomb set to go off at a specific time. When the clock is ticking down and the protagonist or other characters know about it, its effectiveness is tied to the fact that they're fighting that limit. Time is now the obstacle. This is most obvious in thrillers and action films where there is a time limit for specific events and the protagonist is racing against the clock to prevent them. Many James Bond films use this device, complete with the LED clock counting down the seconds to nuclear disaster. But think of *Apollo 13* or *Poseidon*, where the vessels are running out of oxygen to support the characters.

High Noon is an example of the clock being used throughout the entire film to build suspense. The setup for the plot has the bad men who want to kill Will Kane (Gary Cooper) arriving at twelve o'clock noon. Kane tries to assemble help to fight them, but with every failure that finds him closer to the hour of the shootout, he becomes more desperate, and the audience more anxious with him. *Apollo 13, Nick of Time*, and *D.O.A.* all have "big clocks" ticking down to each film's main climax. The tension escalates with the "terrible thing" approaching the characters as they are running out of time to deal with it.

We find a variation of this in *Stranger than Fiction* where we know Karen Eiffel is going to kill off her character at the end of her book, and possibly the real Harold Crick with him. We don't know the exact time death will hit, but we feel it's imminent. Tension builds with our knowledge of this first, and then intensifies when Harold discovers it. Or in *The Terminator*, Sarah Connor (Linda Hamilton) and Kyle Reese (Michael Biehn) are on a collision course with history; the Terminator (Arnold Schwarzenegger) is trying to find and kill her before she can conceive a son who will lead the future resistance.

But shootouts, bombs, and death aren't the only ways to use the clock effectively. Again, the clock is a deadline. Unless the protagonist beats it, something important to the character will be lost or something bad will happen. Think of *The Graduate*. Ben (Dustin Hoffman) is trying to reach Elaine (Katherine Ross) before she says "I do" to another man. This action epitomizes her loss to him. The same strategy has been used in countless movies that end with weddings, from *It Happened One Night* to *My Best Friend's Wedding*, and most recently in *Wedding Crashers*. Instead of it being Claire's wedding, it's her sister's, but the action plays out similarly with John running out of time because Claire is getting closer to her own marriage to Sack. Or look at how the climax of *Liar, Liar* plays out with Fletcher (Jim Carrey) battling the "ticking clock" of an airline departure taking his ex-wife and son away from him.

Besides "big clocks," most films have "scene clocks," where time is running out in a specific scene or sequence. These are deadlines that pertain to relevant, though not climactic, issues within the plot line. These, too, serve to escalate the tension and suspense during the sequence as the audience waits to see how danger is averted or comes to pass. The key here is to play out the beats, showing the fluctuation between the danger and the possibility of warding it off. In *One Flew over the Cuckoo's Nest*, McMurphy wants to watch the baseball playoffs instead of listening to the elevator music that constantly plays on the ward. The playoffs start and end at specific times. Nurse Ratched gives him a chance to see the game if enough of the patients will vote for it, but it's a tie. McMurphy tries to rustle up one more vote before the meeting ends but is unable to; Nurse Ratched declares the meeting over just before the Chief raises his hand, frustrating McMurphy and allowing the audience to feel for him.

Play the Beats

The key to all of this suspense business is to play the beats that pose the most potential danger to your character. Take time to show the problems and conflict as they develop, often leading to more difficult circumstances. This is how you raise the stakes of your story. You let the audience fear the worst for your character, and get him out of the situation by the skin of his teeth. Or let the situation go from bad to worse, and watch that escalate the tension, as subsequent problems must be solved.

Time and again, I see students squander dramatic moments by not playing the conflict. They will set up a potentially gripping situation and then cut away and jump over it, getting to the result to simply move the story on to the next point in the outline. This doesn't build tension and it doesn't involve the audience.

When we see Hooper in *Jaws* slip into the water to examine the wreck that's left of Ben Gardner's boat, we know there's a shark out there. Brody's fear underscores our rising tension as he tries to convince Hooper not to go in but to tow the boat back. But Hooper won't listen; he puts on his gear and swims out. Diving around the boat he finds a big gaping hole in its side. All the while the audience is tense and getting tenser. The suspense mounts. Is the shark going to arrive? Will Hooper survive? Still he takes his time. He examines the hole and finds the shark's tooth, showing it to the audience underwater. Then just when it looks like he's ready to leave Ben Gardner's head rolls into view, scaring Hooper and the audience. They've played the beats, built suspense, and given the audience a shock, just not from what was expected. This brings us to anticipation and surprise.

THE RELATIONSHIP BETWEEN ANTICIPATION AND SURPRISE

Our job as storytellers is to satisfy the audience. Different genres carry varying expectations. But one demand unites all films: YOU CAN'T BE BORING! You must keep your audience engaged, and that means interested, compelled, and entertained. We keep the audience engaged by making sure they understand the action. We accomplish this by creating meaningful relationships between the scenes, building suspenseful sequences that surprise the audience, and allowing the characters' emotional reactions to become part of the plot line. This is really about control. You as the writer are trying to control the audience's experience of your material. To understand this in any other way is to diminish your effectiveness as a screenwriter.

But many writers don't think about what they put on the page beyond the information of the story. They follow a stream of events, taking for granted how their narratives will affect the audience. When a story is defined solely by the plot problem established in the first act, the audience often gets ahead of the film because the action becomes predictable. Sometimes the writers don't recognize the subtext that informs their plots, the questions suggested by the conflict that go unanswered and leave their first audience, the reader, frustrated.

What great writers understand is that from the moment a film or screenplay starts, the audience is always, consciously or unconsciously, trying to get ahead of them. The future of the story is always taking some kind of loose shape in their collective minds. The audience has a natural tendency to anticipate action. It's part of our inherent desire to understand what's happening. We want to know where a story is going and how it will end.

Effective writers take advantage of our propensity to project into the future by using it to shape the audience's experience of the plot action. Take the scene from *Diner* described on page 134. From the moment the two pairs of characters embark upon their collision course for Fenwick's apartment, we are anticipating the disaster that awaits them when they meet up. This creates tension. Because we know how desperate Boogie is, we're willing to bet he's going to bed Beth but keep hoping he won't. Then at the last minute, writer/director Barry Levinson spins the scene with a character revelation, revealing Boogie's better side and surprising us.

This is a really focused sequence that keeps the audience hoping and fearing about the possible outcomes. The screenwriter foreshadows the conflict by crosscutting the two sets of characters with opposing interests, leading the audience to believe they will eventually intersect at a specific destination. The surprise is that the meeting doesn't occur, which reverses the audience's expectations. The bigger surprise, however, is the reason: Boogie's change of heart. *Diner* is filled with these kinds of sequences.

Screenwriters use the relationship between anticipation and surprise to keep the audience from guessing the direction of the story and getting ahead of them. They set up future events for the characters and the audience and then don't give the audience what they expect. When you understand what the audience is anticipating, you can take advantage of it to set up false expectations and misdirect them. You can use these tools to plot a reversal or to create a moment of surprise, to set up a scene, a sequence, or the whole story.

We get the audience anticipating events in a variety of ways. Some expectations are rooted in the goals the protagonist and other main characters have that give a plot its forward momentum. Through the protagonist's interactions with the other characters, goals change and new objectives emerge. In the first half of *E.T.: The Extra-Terrestrial*, Elliott's (Henry Thomas) goal is to hide E.T. and protect him. But in the second half he'll stop at nothing to help him get home. The audience develops expectations around these goals. In the first half of the plot, the audience expects Elliott and E.T. to be discovered and hopes they won't. In the second half, they expect to learn whether Elliott will succeed or fail and what will happen to E.T.

Another way to keep the audience from getting ahead of you is to establish that a specific event is going to happen in a main character's future. Let's say the protagonist meets a woman (beautiful and likeable) and they make a date for the next night. The audience, like the characters, is anticipating that rendezvous. Anytime an important character makes a date, has a deadline, or specifies something they want to accomplish or avoid, you are setting up expectations for the audience that this event is likely to occur. The writer has a choice in how to pay it off. The action can go as planned or develop in a surprising way. If they meet and all goes as planned, something exciting had better follow soon or you're in danger of lulling your audience to sleep. But if something unexpected occurs—they meet, but the woman's boyfriend has followed them—the audience will pay more attention because the event has strayed from their expectations. If the writer forgets about this date and the protagonist never deals with it, the audience will wonder why it was ever mentioned at all and start to lose patience with the story.

Now, obviously, you can't always spin the scenes counter to what the action dictates. But you can turn them enough of the time to keep the audience guessing about where your plot is heading. The key is knowing when to do it and then figuring out how to do it effectively.

Sometimes the audience has inherent expectations owing to the nature of the material. In *Shakespeare in Love*, one of the wonderful things Marc Norman and Tom Stoppard play with is how people with a knowledge of Shakespearean comedy will view the setup of the film. Many of Shakespeare's comedies that use characters masquerading as the opposite sex climax with their exposure. So once Viola dons her mustache to play the part of Thomas, the audience anticipates her reveal at the final climax. When it comes at the top of the second act, it's a surprise and allows the direction of the plot to move in an unexpected way.

In a similar mode, Paul Brickman's *Risky Business* sets up a story that appears to be about a young man losing his virginity. From the moment Joel's friend calls the hooker the audience anticipates this milestone in the teenager's life and probably thinks it will come at the third act climax. But look how the filmmakers play with our expectations. First a transvestite shows up (it's not going to happen with him). But the transvestite gives Joel Lana's number. Then Joel fights with himself about calling her. When he does and she finally shows up, it's before the end of the first act. But now the sex is out of the way, allowing for a new development and the real story we can't predict to take shape for acts two and three.

Sometimes, we set up audience expectations without realizing it. A good test for this is to go through the script scene by scene and determine what questions are left hanging for the audience to wonder about at the end of each one. These uncertainties can create more tension if used properly, and that's just what you have to determine how to do. Another strategy is to query friends and colleagues who first read your script, asking them specifically what they were anticipating at different stages of the story. This can help you to punch up surprises through misdirection and learn if you're telegraphing your story too early.

THE OBLIGATORY SCENE

The idea of the *obligatory scene* was first hit upon by the late-nineteenth-century French critic Francisque Sarcey. He described it as the scene the audience has been waiting for and desires in order for their experience of the story to be fully satisfying. Traditionally, this scene is viewed as the meeting of conflicting forces in the main crisis and climax. In *Jaws*, the principal problem is between shark and sheriff. The obligatory scene, to be satisfying, has to play out between both of them, not between the shark and a giant squid.

Films with clear conflicts between protagonists and antagonists, characterized by a powerful unity of opposites, almost dictate that the main climax plays out between them. Think of *Se7en* without the climax between the detectives and the killer at the last crime scene, or *One Flew over the Cuckoo's Nest* without McMurphy assaulting Nurse Ratched after she's pushed Billy (Brad Dourif) to suicide. If these climaxes left out the characters who represented the main conflict, the endings would feel less than satisfying. Whenever unity of opposites binds the conflicting forces, the climax is obligated to involve the breaking of the bonds that hold them together.

There are some films, however, in which the main problems are not necessarily set up between characters in a protagonist/antagonist relationship. In *Jerry Maguire*, Jerry's struggled through a series of conflicts in trying to find meaning as well as success not only in his career but his life. That greater goal continually eludes him, and as the climax approaches, Dorothy leaves him. When the climax comes at the football game, Jerry's a spectator to the events. Rod Tidwell gets hit and goes down, and with him everything Jerry's worked for—the contract, his agency, his life. We fear with Jerry it's all over. And then Tidwell gets up, the crowd goes wild, and Jerry is overcome with emotion. But he still doesn't feel complete.

Although the second half of the plot has been built around Jerry and Tidwell chasing Rod's contract, just closing the deal wouldn't be an adequate ending for Jerry's story. Jerry wants a meaningful life; he wants not only a great career but also the loving, honest, and supportive relationship that Tidwell and his wife, Marcee (Regina King), have. He has to resolve his intimacy problems with Dorothy to find real significance and value in life and make his success worthwhile. The events he witnesses push him back to Dorothy, and he finally expresses his feelings to her, thus giving the audience the satisfying ending they desire. In this sense, Jerry has to experience business success without Dorothy to realize the value of their relationship. This development defines the theme of the film.

The obligatory scene, then, is tied to your theme as well as your conflict. It is where you prove your premise through how the crisis at the climax tests your protagonist, allowing you to dramatize the change your character has experienced (or has failed to experience).

There is one other point to take into consideration here. Sometimes a film sets up an idea in the audience's mind that must be dealt with in some fashion, even though it's not the main conflict. The idea has resonated throughout the plot so strongly that it has to be resolved. *American Beauty* and *Monster's Ball* both raise intense issues that percolate around the main conflict. In *American Beauty*, it's Lester's fantasy about Angela. In *Monster's Ball*, it's what will happen when Leticia (Halle Berry) finally discovers that Hank (Billy Bob Thornton) participated in the execution of her husband. Although both films deal with other conflicts and resolve them, these questions are so powerful that if they weren't answered, the audience would feel unsatisfied and their experience of each film would be unfulfilling.

What was really potent about both these, and all great climaxes, is that the writers and filmmakers found unexpected ways to deliver what they'd promised the audience. In *American Beauty*, Lester can have Angela, but he won't take her when she reveals she's a virgin. In *Monster's Ball*, Leticia does learn Hank was at her husband's execution. Hurt and betrayed, not only by Hank's failure to disclose this fact but also by his father's actions toward her, she goes to confront him. She finds him unaware that anything's changed, simply enjoying ice cream that he offers to share with her, free from his father, free to be with her. In this moment she melts, seeing the good man in him despite this one failing. Both endings come as surprises that complete the stories in fulfilling ways.

A great climax is what you set up and promise your audience in terms of the conflicts your characters face. It should be exciting, startling, and moving. It can be provocative. It must be riveting. But it can't play out the way your audience expects it; there has to be something unexpected, unforeseen to really satisfy your audience.

CHAPTER 8

COMMON PROBLEMS IN PLOT CONSTRUCTION

Writing a screenplay is a tricky business. No matter how much time you spend working out the details before going to script, there will always be difficulties. The conflict we rely on to create our stories comes and confronts us in the form of writer's block. Then there's the dreadful reality of rewriting. Yet all writing depends on this process of revision to clarify ideas.

Screenwriting is a long arduous process, not for the faint of heart, and only for those steadfast in their commitment to their characters and ready to tackle the problems that will lead to better work. But the trick is being able to identify those trouble areas in the script and then decide how to address them. Here are some common problems writers encounter and how to recognize and overcome them.

SCRIPTS OVERPLOTTED IN ACTION

One of the most common problems many scripts have is that they are overplotted in terms of the action. This means they're so filled with incident that the reader never gets a sense of the characters or what the story means beyond the plot problem. Generally, when screenplays are overplotted in action, they're underplotted in characterizations. Scenes aren't used to show how the conflict affects the characters. Instead we're whisked through the events, and the meaning of it all is lost on us.

Scenes Need to Show the Effect of Conflict on the Characters

One of the main points of this book is that meaning is developed through the effect conflict has on the characters. If we don't know how the conflict affects them, we don't if it's important enough to warrant our own interest. The conflict—the problem the protagonist and other characters face—has to be vitally important to them for it to affect us. And we have to see this to know it. *The plot must include scenes that show the effect conflict has on the characters*. Remember, this also adds to our understanding of who each character really is.

But this is only the starting point. How you reveal the character's response to the conflict and action must be real and interesting in and of itself. This is where you may run into problems. If there is too much plot action to be played, the room left for character response will be limited. You won't have the time or space to come up with interesting and motivated character scenes.

In the last chapter we discussed a short sequence from *Erin Brockovich* that shows Erin's reaction to losing her job (a setback). She takes her anger out on George (and the cockroach) but ultimately allows him to comfort her. He comes into her life as a result. The scene that follows her outburst shows them connecting and the audience learns a little of her back story. It offers a softer side of Erin, and as Erin and George bond, the audience bonds with them.

The point of this development in the plot is to show the growing relationship between Erin and George as one that will be threatened by other developments later in the story. Because we care about the characters and their connection, we're drawn deeper into the film. In this group of scenes, nothing is wasted. Everything is used to make relevant points that bear on the way we understand the development of the material.

In another film, a character's response to the conflict might create a whole sequence that pulls the audience in and defines the character. In *Amelie,* a sequence starts when Amelie (Audrey Tautou) discovers her neighbor, the corner grocer, has left his keys in his apartment door. Through her action, going to return the keys, the audience sees a good deed about to be done. But when Amelie watches the grocer berate his one-armed employee for taking too much time with the customers, she looks at the keys and retreats. The filmmakers, director and co-writer Jean-Pierre Jeunet and screenwriter Guillaume Laurant, show her response to this unkindness. Amelie makes a copy of the key, returns the original to its lock, and then at the right time, she sneaks into the neighbor's apartment and creates mischief. In his bedroom, she takes his alarm clock, set for 7 A.M., and resets it for four in the morning. In the bathroom, she finds a tube of foot cream and switches it with his toothpaste. Each step shows her thinking about her action, giving the audience time to imagine what she might do with the items, what they might do. When she compares the foot cream to the toothpaste, the audience knows exactly what's going on in her mind before she completes the action. Plus, the longer she's in his apartment, the more tension the audience feels, knowing the neighbor could come back at any moment. She does this not once, but twice, causing the grocer's nerves to fray. The audience takes surreptitious pleasure in her actions, participating and identifying with her every step of the way, and it draws them deeper into the story.

Both of these episodes reveal characterizations created through action. The actions come in response to other dramatic incidents. They take time to develop. They allow the audience time to process the information and feel with the character, making them participants in the story, rather than simply spectators.

As you go through your plot, look at the scenes where your main characters actively work toward their objectives. When the sequence climaxes, do they succeed or fail? What does their success or failure mean in the broader context of the story? What would their reaction tell the audience about what has just happened? Then you have to determine if the reaction adds or detracts to overall effect of your work.

Create Meaningful Action and Not Merely Activity

Another sign of overplotting is when there are numerous scenes showing characters "doing" what they do. As we write these scenes, we believe we're demonstrating who a character is through all her actions, like work or hobbies. For example, my protagonist is a medical student, so I show her attending a lecture in medical school. She's studious, so I show her studying. She's a good person, so I show her giving to the Red Cross. She's going crazy, so I show her standing on her head at a concert. These are all written as separate scenes. I think I'm showing a multidimensional character, but the actions play like "business," or mere activity, because they aren't made meaningful to the reader. The actions aren't developed to have any effect on the character's relationships or goals.

What we need is meaningful action. These are the steps the characters take that cost or gain them something as they strive toward their goals. This is action that shows who the character is as a result of what they pursue or avoid.

How do we create meaningful action? It depends on what your story is about. Maybe one of your main characters is a real estate agent, but her career isn't really part of the story, which is about a disintegrating marriage. You're just including it to show what she does for a living, *who* she is. You write a scene where she shows a house. There, you think, it's out of the way. But it really has no impact. Now remember the scene in *American Beauty* in which Carolyn shows the house. Alan Ball is more concerned with the effect it has on her, and *this* is what shows us who she is. He could have picked any job for Carolyn and written a scene that made us understand her self-loathing through what she does. But he goes further; he uses her occupation through the developments with Buddy Kane, the Real Estate King. Buddy represents the success Carolyn craves. Her lunch with him leads to their affair, exposing yet another side of Carolyn's character and affecting the plot in her betrayal of her husband, Lester. Mr. Ball works the information into the plot of the story so that it has meaning and impact. There isn't a wasted moment of screen time.

This is what great writers do. They understand that everything they show has to have relevance; it all has to connect for the viewer to put the information of the story together properly. It goes back to cause-and-effect plotting. If we want the audience to appreciate and follow the information, as well as the action to build momentum, scenes need to affect the subsequent scenes. They have to be related (see Chapter 4, The Principles of Action).

Signs of Overplotting

An indication of overplotting is when readers don't "get" what your screenplay is about. They can't grasp the characters or the theme. This can also be the result of not enough happening in a script. But if you have a strong conflict driving the plot, overplotting could be the problem. If it is, you want to look specifically at what this conflict means to you and your characters. Nine times out of ten, writers know what it means; they have just left out the scenes that show the protagonist's and other main characters' reactions to the conflict. The next step is to incorporate your characters' responses to the conflict in scenes that show how they're affected.

What if, to do a great job including these responses in your story, you now have a screenplay that's too long? This is the toughest part of screenwriting—cutting things out. But that's what you have to do. You have to become ruthless. Look at your script carefully and remove everything that isn't pertinent to your main conflict. You need to work out where you can telescope the action and create bridges between your sequences. If you know what your story is really about, the choices will become clear to you.

PEOPLE CAN'T RELATE—WHY?

Overplotting can be a reason why readers can't relate to your material. But there are other causes, too.

The Conflict Isn't Tracking

Conflict needs to develop and *track*. This is the basis of cause-and-effect plotting. To follow along, the audience has to understand what's happening and why. Conflict doesn't generally just drop into a reader's lap fully formed at the start of a screenplay. (Obviously, a writer needs to fully understand it, but one rarely starts out with a story's conflict completely developed in the first scene. Even though *Jaws* starts with a shark attack, the first hurdle Chief Brody has to get across is city hall.) Conflict has causes and sources and produces consequences and effects. Look at a great film and you'll see how the filmmakers set up conflict early to hook the audience. Then they develop it into another related and more important conflict that causes new and more serious problems. Throughout these ensuing problems, the filmmakers track the main conflict, showing its progression through the action until finally all the problems come together and must be dealt with at the climax.

In *Shakespeare in Love*, Will starts with a problem: writer's block. He needs money and he can't write a play. It turns out his writer's block is connected to his love life; his muse is another man's mistress. Even though Rosaline (Sandra Reinton) is romantically linked to Burbage (Martin Clunes), she persuades Will that she loves only him, and he breaks through the block. But when she betrays him with yet another man and Will hears his rival Kit Marlowe's (Rupert Everett) play is to premiere at Burbage's theater instead of his, he burns his work and sinks further into depression.

Committed to putting something on at the Rose, he starts with the actors, regardless of having no play written. He meets Viola, who comes masquerading as a boy, Thomas, to join the players. Thinking Thomas is his Romeo, he causes Viola as Thomas to panic and run off. Will chases her back to her estate where he sees Viola as herself and finds his true muse. His writer's block is fixed, and now he can really write. But this creates a new problem: Wessex, Viola's fiancé, and the villain of the film.

A chain of problems arises in act one, revealing what's at the core of the film—a love story in the traditional "boy meets girl, boy loses girl" format. The audience can clearly see how one event leads to another, in the orchestration of the conflict through cause-and-effect plotting.

In act two we see Will and Viola's love grow, and along with it, the play. But with her impending marriage, Wessex's jealousy, and the fact that Will's already married, we know we're in for a bumpy ride. All this is wonderfully tracked, along with several other subplots that include Will's rivalry with Marlowe, Henslowe and Fennyman's relationship, and the contention between Burbage's Curtain Theater and the Rose. Finally, by the end of act two, Viola is revealed as Thomas, the play is shut down, forcing the lovers to part, and the Rose Theater is closed.

Act three brings Burbage to the rescue of Will's play. But this action doesn't stop Viola's marriage to Wessex. Even so, she escapes to see the play before sailing off to the New World. Will fills in as Romeo, but Sam's (Daniel Brocklebank) voice has changed and they have no one to play Juliet—until Viola appears to take the part. The result is a triumph of theater-making. When Wessex is just about to reveal their ruse, the queen (Judi Dench) steps in and saves the lovers. She rewards Will by naming him the winner of a bet about love placed with Wessex in act one, but she can't undo the marriage. In the end, Will loses Viola but retains her inspiration, as Viola lives on in his imagination.

This is a wonderful example of how the conflicts develop and escalate to a surprising yet satisfying conclusion. Although the conflicts are actualized in events, they are built on the characters' feelings and relationships. These provide the motivations and the reactions that are incorporated into the plot, so that the audience understands all along what is happening and why. If you reread the synopses of *Se7en* and *American Beauty* in Chapter 6, The Sequence of Story, you'll see two more examples of how conflict tracks.

When conflict either doesn't develop or does so without clear character motivations and desires, the plot action becomes harder for the audience to relate to because they don't understand why things are happening. The sequence of events lacks clarity, making the stories confusing and causing story momentum to break down. The audience is given too much information to follow and retain.

The basis of a great movie is a simple story that is well developed in terms of 1) the actions taken in the face of the conflict and 2) how the conflict affects the main characters. *Shakespeare in Love* has a clear central conflict with numerous characters swirling around the theater and the play. Even a film such as *Nashville*, which has twenty-two different characters involved in almost as many subplots, is relatively easy to understand. It plays against the backdrop of a presidential campaign. Everything happening in the film revolves around it, and this gives the audience a way to understand all of the stories as they unfold.

If a poorly tracked conflict is your problem, look at how you've positioned your main conflict in your story. Is it central to the development of the plot? Is it tracking through the story, progressing and escalating in a way we clearly understand? Check to make sure you're showing the effects the conflict has on the characters, especially the setbacks. Does their suffering reflect the costs? This will help a reader or viewer to understand what the conflict means to the characters and allow her to empathize with them.

The Character Arc Isn't Tracking

If you look at *Shakespeare in Love* carefully, you'll see how each character arc progresses and develops through the plot. Will begins the film blocked and unhappy. Although he ends miserable, he's no longer blocked; he's writing again. He's connected with his inner muse, who will continue to inspire him. Viola begins as a naïve young woman wanting the romance of the theater. She ends as a woman who has had a great love and, despite the marriage of convenience for her parents' sake, will be stronger for it. The plot manages this by keeping the two principals close to the flames of conflict, forcing them to make decisions, take action, and feel disappointment as well as joy.

(Again, a review of the synopses of *Se7en* and *American Beauty* in Chapter 6 illustrates how character arcs track.)

Characters' emotions need to be developed believably for an audience to understand them. This orchestration must be motivated and real. It advances a step at a time, through action and reaction. If characters jump from one emotion to another, with no clear progression, they become hard to understand. You need to show the reasons for a character's transformation throughout a story. A character's reaction to shocking news might at first be disbelief. Later on, it might turn to anger, then to depression and despair, before the character comes to acceptance. Your audience will understand the character better if you take the time to reveal her experiences.

The Exposition Isn't Tracking

Remember, exposition is information. When the exposition doesn't track, your story breaks down because the information links aren't working. This frequently happens in mysteries, thrillers, and investigative genres, which require the audience to access information and clues to make the proper connections and understand what's going on. Sometimes writers feel they're being too obvious with these details and so they bury them in a scene. But this only frustrates the reader. If a writer sets up a question, and then starts the next scene as though the question had never been raised, he may destroy scene continuity and story momentum because the meaning gets lost.

Tracking the exposition means understanding what information the audience needs to grasp, scene by scene, and when to give it out for them to follow the plot. If a scene raises a specific question for the reader, in most cases, it's important to handle it soon, preferably in the next scene. It needs to be answered, developed, or pushed off. But it must be dealt with so your reader doesn't think it's been forgotten. If the question is important, it should be taken care of directly in the following scene so the reader will keep that information handy to put together with other parts of the story.

Let's say a scene ends with your protagonist saying, "I wonder what happened to Johnny?" Your next scene doesn't have to show Johnny. But if the missing Johnny is important to the plot *and* the protagonist, and the next scene features your protagonist, you should probably deal with this question. One way might be to show the protagonist considering something belonging to Johnny at the top of the scene before moving on to other points. This way the audience knows Johnny is still on his mind, even if they don't know where the elusive character is. What's key is to carry the continuity of the previous scene into the following one.

A common mishandling of exposition has a character trying to find something out (i.e., he wants information and the audience *needs* this information). A scene establishes this and reveals which character has that information. In the next scene, the two characters make small talk for more than a couple of pages. By the time they get to the "question," the reader is so pissed off, he couldn't care less about it because the discussion has diminished the importance of the information. Now, if this scene were to be filmed, the editor would cut away all the chit-chat (unless it was purposeful and full of conflict) to start the scene as close to the "answer" as he could. But, as I said above, writers often feel they're being too obvious, so they hide the information, and their scripts suffer for it when readers get frustrated.

Some movies need information to be laid out for the audience so they understand what's happening and why. Look at *Erin Brockovich* again and you'll see that the numerous exposition scenes are clear and specific. They're handled in a way that seems natural for the characters. And even if the audience doesn't catch every nuance, they understand enough to stay with the story as it develops. This is what makes "The Plan" such a useful exposition tool.

In a movie, though, a viewer must glean the facts from what they see and hear. The audience can't go back and reread a passage they don't understand the way they can in a book. The story has to be clear the first viewing. Although your first audience is a reader, professional story analysts are trained to read a script as if it is a movie. If they constantly have to double-check the information to understand what's happening, they become frustrated and usually pass on the material. A script needs to unfold for the reader to give him the experience of the movie.

There are always exceptions. Ensemble and nonlinear films are the most obvious. They often end a segment of one storyline with a question, like a cliffhanger, then pick up the threads of another subplot to develop before coming back to deal with the first one. If subplots are clearly developed in scenes plotted with strong cause-and-effect relationships, the audience can keep them straight. But when they aren't, if the critical questions your audience is left wondering about aren't tracked, then the subplots start to unravel into a tangle of threads.

Using a Task to Keep the Story on Track

One way to help your reader stay connected with your screenplay is to use a task that has to be done to create continuity of action. The task could be the play in *Shakespeare in Love*; it's what the protagonist and other characters must accomplish. The story revolves around it. It creates purposeful action, allowing your audience to plug into basic meaning; it also helps build tension. In *The Wizard of Oz*, Dorothy wants to get home, but she has several things she must accomplish before that can happen. She has to get to Oz. Once in Oz, the wizard sends her to get the witch's broomstick.

Most plots are constructed using tasks to drive portions of the action. In *Se7en*, making sense of the crime scenes is the first step to finding the killer. In *Tootsie*, there are rehearsals for the soap opera; in *Pulp Fiction*, Vincent (John Travolta) and Jules (Samuel L. Jackson) have a briefcase to recover and the boss's wife to take care of, and other things to do as well.

Tasks set up audience expectations about what action will take place and what it will produce. An audience follows a character with something to do and on a basic level wonders if he will get it done. Tension develops with that. The harder the task is to accomplish, the more tension it can generate, as long as the character cares what happens, and there's some worry over his success or failure.

The task can carry the weight of an entire plot, even as it's divided up into smaller increments of action. In *Apollo 13*, the astronauts' task is to get home, but to do so there are numerous jobs they must complete. In the *Se7en* and the *Die Hard* series, the policemen's goal is to solve the criminal problems. In *The African Queen*, Rose (Katharine Hepburn) and Charlie (Humphrey Bogart) are trying to get the *Queen* down the Ulanga River to torpedo the German gunship, the *Louisa*. In *His Girl Friday*, Walter Burns (Cary Grant) tricks his ex-wife and former ace reporter Hildy (Rosalind Russell) into covering one last big story in order to win her back from her new fiancé, Bruce (Ralph Bellamy). But the task can also be used more provisionally, as in *American Beauty*. Here, tasks are smaller in scope: Lester working out to make himself attractive to Angela or Carolyn's affair with Buddy can be considered tasks. These are the specific actions in which they're engaged.

A task can also be used to lead into and set in motion larger action, creating continuity and tension. Many new writers often create a scenario that has numerous characters to introduce and important exposition to get across before they can get to the main problem/conflict where the plot really engages, at the end of act one. But these scenes will leave the reader feeling as though nothing's happening. He will start to get impatient and lose interest. However, if you craft a line of action in which one character has something to accomplish, and throw problems in his way, you can produce enough tension to carry your reader along until the major conflict of the plot starts. The key, again, is to make the problem important enough to the character; that will lead your reader to become involved.

UNDERSTANDING WHEN THE AUDIENCE KNOWS WHAT

It's very important to consider fully the pace at which your first audience—the reader—can put together the sense of your story. It's easy to assume that the reader gets the information you've planted as it comes up in dialogue and specific actions. However, your words aren't all the reader brings to the table; his own life experiences, intuitions, and intelligence all come to bear on how he perceives your project. He calls upon this when he's attempting to follow the logic and meaning of your story. However, you can't possibly anticipate the specific perspective of each individual reader. This is why, if you intend to surprise him, you need to pay very close attention to what he's learning in every scene and how he might add it up along the way.

The challenge here is that a great film allows the audience to experience the story along with the characters. This means the audience feels the characters' emotions, thinks their thoughts, and figures out parts of the story with them along the way. When this happens, you create a real sense of participation in the audience. It's not just your story; it's *their* story, too.

But this doesn't mean the audience figures out *everything*. They have to be surprised (as does your protagonist) for the script and film to work. Writers have a fine line to walk, between giving the audience too much and too little. If you tell too much information, the audience figures everything out before you want them to; tell too little, and they don't have enough to hang onto, so they stop caring about the action and fail to become truly involved.

What's a writer to do?

As you consider the plot of your script, you have to think about each scene from the point of view of your reader and know what you want her to think throughout your plot. What is each scene supposed to accomplish in terms of exposition, emotion, characterization, suspense, and momentum? For example, in a mystery, you need to anticipate whom your audience is logically going to suspect as the perpetrator of the crime. If he is actually your culprit, then you have to *plot* to make the audience think otherwise. You need to focus scenes and action that throw the suspicion on another character to divert the reader. That's what effective writers do. When they want to surprise the reader, they misdirect him and often slip in a twist that he, along with the characters, can't expect.

This is difficult for new writers to master, but it's absolutely necessary. Your first reads can help you. When you finish a draft of your script, you have to get it read. You might not have a handy script consultant at your service, but you will have colleagues, family, and friends who'll consent to read your project. When they do, you need them to be honest with you about their experience of the material. Most people won't understand the finer points of screenwriting, but that's not what's important. Your first readers don't have to be screenplay savvy to help. All they have to do is give you their reactions. Ask them if they could follow along. Did they feel tension? If the script felt slow, can they remember where? If they anticipated where you were going before you got there, ask them to pinpoint when those intuitions first surfaced. You need to quiz them on their hunches and suspicions about your characters and your plot's developments and final outcome. If they are getting ahead of your plotting and figuring out too soon where your story is headed, then you know you need to go back to the drawing board.

When the audience gets ahead of you, it can also mean the conflict isn't high enough. You're not putting a sufficient amount of stress into the lives of your characters, making the story too obvious. If this is the case, you need to consider if things aren't too easy for your protagonist. Maybe you need more negative outcomes to the obstacles and complications he confronts. Real conflict pressures your characters with troubling options and casts deep doubt on whether your protagonist can succeed. When the audience doesn't know what will happen, and feels that more than one outcome is possible, they're unlikely to jump ahead with certainty.

TO-ING AND FRO-ING: USING TOO MANY BEATS TO ACCOMPLISH THE TASK

Another common problem many scripts suffer from is what I call "to-ing and fro-ing." This is when the action seesaws back and forth between scenes too many times in a sequence. Characters go to the same locales, playing the same beats and refusing to take action. While this may be an accurate portrait of life, it's troublesome in plotting. It tends to create action that feels repetitive, makes characters seem passive, and bores the audience.

Movement must lead somewhere. Even if a character vacillates in the plot before committing to a course of action, these shifts need to be played in such a way that they don't wear thin the audience's patience. Generally, we move through these beats of the story quickly, to get to more definitive action.

To-ing and fro-ing is easy to spot in a script. You look for the places in the screenplay where characters go back and forth between the same locations. For example: Your protagonist Jack is at home and calls his wayward girlfriend Jill, who isn't at her place. He goes to her house anyway and knocks. She's not there, so he goes home. At home she calls him and tells him to come over. He returns to her house to learn she's leaving him. This action takes five beats to communicate that Jack's girlfriend is dumping him. This could easily be trimmed to one or two scenes.

Wherever you seem to be going back and forth between locations, look hard and see if you can do it one step instead of three. If you need more than one, will two do? You're looking to build firm action, action with a purpose that leads somewhere—somewhere where something will happen.

This doesn't mean that you never go back to a location once you've used it. To the contrary. It means you make good use of it when you do go there again.

THE PASSIVE PROTAGONIST: MOVING FROM CONFLICTED TO COMPELLING

A studio reader once told me that the most common problem rejected scripts have is a passive protagonist. This protagonist just doesn't want anything and so he doesn't act. Or if he does want something, his desire is too abstract to drive a plot. I understand the attraction of the antihero, the character who is disaffected by life. But for him to be dramatically productive—to create a compelling story—he must be active.

Remember, we're using the language of drama to tell our stories. This language demands that characters actively engage with others, want something, take action, and meet with conflict, to make the story interesting to us as we watch. The audience needs the protagonist, and other main characters, to pursue their desires for us to get involved with them. In books, language can carry us. But in film, action and conflict create interest.

To use an alienated character as your protagonist, one who has disengaged from the world, you must get her to respond dramatically to a situation. You have to provoke her to act. You need to create a condition, set of circumstances, or problem big enough to draw a response from her so that she becomes a *reactive* protagonist. Think of Lester in *American Beauty*. At the beginning of the movie, he's frustrated, disgruntled, unhappy, and henpecked. But once his fantasy about his daughter's friend engages, he reacts and creates action and conflict for the audience to follow. Or look at Bobby Dupea in *Five Easy Pieces*. In the setup, the film establishes who Bobby is: the hotheaded oil-rigger in California's central valley who can't commit. Bobby is plenty conflicted, just as Lester is, but he isn't goal driven until he gets word from his sister that his father is sick and he needs to come home. Now the story really starts, about this character who has to return to face something he wants to avoid. The film *The Station Agent* features a protagonist who only wants to be left alone. You can't get much more passive that this. But what confronts him? Two characters who are desperately lonely and insist on being with him.

In character-oriented screenplays, sometimes the main conflict is not entirely evident to the writer, and so it can't be clear to the reader. Often the script pulls you along for a while with interesting characters but loses steam because the writer hasn't provided enough focus on this centralized problem. The protagonist drifts through the story, surrounded by funny or appealing characters, but he doesn't act, and story momentum breaks down.

With these stories you need to uncover the character's real problem, and whom it's with. You must dig deeply into him and find out why he's disaffected and what his internal conflict is.

Academy Award–winning screenwriter Robert Towne has said that when he knows what his character is afraid of, he knows what the character has to face. This is as good a place as any to start. A character's fear can be used to define not only who he is but also the action he must pursue. This conflict can become the spine of your story while you explore the other issues and characters that make your screenplay unique and interesting. We'll talk more about this in the next chapter.

CHAPTER 9

TOOLS FOR ANALYSIS

When a screenplay's not working, we can beat our heads against the wall trying to figure out why. Friends and colleagues may give conflicting thoughts and reasons, but, often, no one will be able to tell you exactly where your script has gone wrong. Although there's no absolute, surefire way to diagnose a project's problems, there are a few principles you can apply to assess and gauge what's not working and what needs to be done. Let's look at them.

DISCOVERING THE PASSIVE PROTAGONIST

Whenever you get feedback saying your script feels slow, lacks tension, and readers can't tell what it's about, you have to consider whether you have a passive protagonist. This can also be the result of too little conflict. But if your hero is wandering through the pages of your screenplay without purpose, chances are her passivity is the problem.

From the first chapter on, this book has done nothing if it hasn't sold you on this basic principle of screenwriting: Protagonists must be active. They have to be driven to pursue their goals, even if it's to be left alone, á la Rick in *Casablanca* or Finbar McBride (Peter Dinklage) in *The Station Agent*. They must be striving to get what they want, or the reader will wonder why he's supposed to be interested in this character. Why should he care about someone who's wasting time just hanging out? Unless they are hysterically funny, characters who float around in a story test our patience and ultimately fail to hold our interest.

To find out if this is your problem, go through your script and identify the scenes where your protagonist is active. This means she wants and/or is trying to accomplish something. Count them up. Then pinpoint the scenes where your character is passive. These are the points where she's an observer while other characters around her take action. If the scenes where your protagonist is a bystander outnumber the scenes where she's active and involved, you probably have a passive protagonist.

In the last chapter, I talked about provoking a character to take action, and this is vital. Another solution is to find ways to make your protagonist central to the action. She must be the driving force of the plot, pushing the action from scene to scene. Look at the other characters who are active. Often we find these secondary characters more interesting than the protagonist because their action makes them more dynamic. You want to ask yourself: Can any of these actions be given to your protagonist? If so, do it and adapt the scenes to accommodate your hero.

You won't be able to give all the important action to your protagonist, but she needs to make the major contribution in the scenes to be the driving force of the plot. In the scenes where she must remain a bystander, find her reaction to what's happening. Ask yourself how to make that reaction a focal point in the scene. How will you convey the emotion? This will help the reader track the meaning of what he's seeing your protagonist experience.

The active protagonist in pursuit of her objectives will help define the basic meaning of your story, leading your reader to understand it on this fundamental plot level. The attention you pay to your character's reactions to what happens and what she learns will further define the audience's understanding, leading them to the deeper meaning of your material—i.e., the theme.

Identifying the scenes where your protagonist is active and passive is not only helpful when analyzing a screenplay; it's a particularly powerful tool to use when you've completed an outline. Applying this technique during the outlining stage can save a writer a lot of time and energy.

IDENTIFYING THE CORE CONFLICT TO SERVE AS THE STORY SPINE

Sometimes writers set up characters in a situation and just let them interact, building (they hope) to a big payoff scene where they expose the true meaning of their story. Other times writers follow a character on a journey, observing him move from place to place, meet people, do and learn things. Either of these strategies is problematic and often leads readers to remark that the script feels slow, they don't understand the character's problem, and aren't sure what it's all about. Generally, the audience doesn't have the patience to wait two hours for that one explosive scene to come or to follow a character going from place to place without knowing why. We need tension and action, conflict and direction, to create meaning. We need to understand the conflict as it develops, along with the characters' reactions to it.

Getting this kind of feedback can be a sign that the story has no true focus and the conflict isn't clear, even though it may be clear to you. What your script could need is a spine or frame to hold all the parts together and bring them into relationship. In most cases, the plot spine is a conflict that clearly states the protagonist's problem and what's at stake for him and creates a desire that forces movement. Another, simpler way to grasp this is to ask: What does my protagonist really want and what's stopping him from getting it? You must be able to articulate this conflict to make it work for you.

A common misunderstanding new writers have about the plot spine is that it defines the whole work. This isn't so. Often the spine is used to delineate the parameters of the conflict and set up stakes that have to be paid off by the end. Then the writer explores the real issue of the story, the one that's important to her, in relationship to this conflict. *Rain Man*, *American Beauty*, and *Monster's Ball* all use core conflicts to create a dynamic structure within which the story may function. Think of the director of the institution who controls Charlie's father's estate in *Rain Man*. The use of this character creates narrative boundaries and allows Charlie and Raymond's relationship, the real point of the story, to develop within it. In the end, when his connection to Raymond has become meaningful to Charlie, this conflict rises again to threaten its depth. Look at *American Beauty*. The story is about a man whose infatuation with his daughter's friend wakes him up and compels him to change. This fixation threatens his family relationships, with his wife and daughter. But within it, the film comments on what makes a meaningful life. *Monster's Ball* is about a former prison guard's relationship with the widow whose husband he had a hand in executing. The real story is about confronting family values around a father/son conflict, first between Hank Grotowski and his son, Sonny (Heath Ledger), and then between Hank and his own father, Buck (Peter Boyle).

The spine, or core conflict, gives a plot form and helps ground the reader in the problem that will serve as the container of the story. When using this kind of spine, you must remember to deal with and use it, coming back to it during the course of the action and in or around your climax. There you must answer the dramatic question set up for the audience in the first act so this structural strategy pays off in a satisfying way.

IDENTIFYING POSITIVE AND NEGATIVE SCENE VALUES

When readers feel the script is slow and lacks tension, the cause isn't always a passive protagonist or the lack of a central conflict. It could be a problem with how you've developed the opposition your hero faces. You just might've made things too easy for him, and the conflict, in the form of the antagonist and obstacles, isn't strong enough. A protagonist needs real opposition to build tension and produce worry in the audience over his fate. When problems are solved too readily, there's no reason to fret. The audience starts expecting events to go the hero's way and loses interest in what happens.

Remember, conflict develops positively and negatively to create tension and suspense (see Chapter 3, p. 37). The protagonist has to experience both successes and setbacks. Where real tension builds, protagonists fail, time and again, casting doubt on whether they can really complete their tasks and attain their goals.

To find out if this is causing the breakdown in your script, go back through your work scene by scene and identify the positive and negative values. These are the scene outcomes, the results of your character's encounters with the obstacles and complications, which you can quantify as good, bad, or neutral. If there are more good and neutral outcomes, where things go your protagonist's way, than bad ones, then this is probably the trouble. Things are working out too well for your hero to generate anxiety in your audience.

There are several things you can do. First, reconsider the opposition in your story and look for ways to strengthen it. Do you have a principal antagonist? If not, if you created one would it foster more conflict by having a chief adversary who can work consciously to thwart the hero? This can be a powerful tool, bringing the opposition your protagonist must face into clear focus. The audience will be more likely to understand the clash in the opposing desires and anticipate a winner and loser.

If you have an antagonist already, ask yourself if, at the start, he is stronger, smarter, and better equipped than the protagonist for the ordeal? Or is he just a straw man—someone easily overcome? If he isn't a real danger to your hero's success, he doesn't contribute to the tension level, in which case you have to ask why he is there. You need to build up this type of antagonist and give him real power to make him dramatically productive.

An antagonist doesn't have to rule the show, but he can contribute to the tension level in different sections of a plot by focusing the conflict between him and your hero. Remember how Cameron Crowe uses Bob Sugar in *Jerry Maguire*. He functions as an antagonist at the end of act one and throughout the first part of act two. Then he disappears for a while, only to rise again at the end of act three.

If your story doesn't use an antagonist, then you need to look at the hero's problem. Is this conflict too small to be difficult for him to overcome? Maybe it just isn't significant enough to warrant all the fuss? If it isn't testing and threatening the protagonist with failure or worse, then it's not doing its job. The obstacles and complications must cause your hero trauma—not just hassle him. They have to jeopardize everything that he holds dear.

IDENTIFYING THE KEY RELATIONSHIP THE AUDIENCE CAN ROOT FOR

You finish your script, and get it Xeroxed, then bound. You work your connections to get it read. You wait patiently for feedback to come in, and brace yourself for it. Your reader finally gets back to you. He says, although he found the script interesting, he really couldn't get into it. You prod him further and it comes out: He couldn't care less about your protagonist. And if he can't care about him, it's hard to care about the story.

Apathy for the protagonist from the reader is another common problem screenplays suffer. The cause of this can be a passive protagonist. But if the hero is actively pursuing objectives and goals and meeting with conflict, then there has to be another reason. When a writer gets this criticism about a story with a clearly active protagonist, she often tries to solve it by crafting a tragic back story—one she feels is poignant and moving. Then she looks for ways to tell this sad story, in dialogue, thinking it will make the reader feel empathy for the protagonist. Sometimes it's interesting. More often, it's just depressing and does very little to induce goodwill on the part of the reader and make him care.

When there's plenty of action for the hero, and apathy for the character is the problem, it's generally produced not because the protagonist lacks a sad story but because he functions throughout the plot alone. He has his mission; he single-handedly takes action in pursuit of his goal, he meets with conflict and handles it solo, and then succeeds or fails by himself. What this hero lacks is a meaningful relationship.

Protagonists need to affect other characters to move the audience. We need to see them care about others and others care about them. Rick, in *Casablanca*, who famously says "I stick my neck out for no one," shows his feelings for the people in his life, from his employees to his ex-girlfriend Yvonne, through how he deals with them. And they show their feelings for him through the respect and dedication they give in return. As we the audience watch a movie, we vicariously live through the characters. We hope for the best for them and fear the worst. Just as in our own lives we want to find positive relationships, we hope they will find these in theirs so that we can feel the connections through them.

If your story is missing a key relationship for your protagonist, you need to find one. It's very difficult to write a compelling screenplay if your characters don't connect. Emotions are strongest when they're shared. Even the makers of *Cast Away* had to invent Wilson the Volleyball for Chuck (Tom Hanks) to interact with. For many movies, the "love" interest serves this purpose, whether it's consummated or unrequited. But don't think falling in love with the opposite sex (or same for that matter) is the only way for your protagonist to connect. A core relationship can be between any individuals who share a meaningful bond. Think of Charlie and Raymond in *Rain Man*, or Ratzo Rizzo (Dustin Hoffman) and Joe Buck (Jon Voight) in *Midnight Cowboy*, or Harry (Daniel Radcliffe), Ron (Rupert Grint), and Hermione (Emma Watson) in any of the *Harry Potter* films. Stories work best when they're about people affecting other people. Relationships give stories depth and help to create stakes and make us care.

After receiving this type of criticism, how do you go about creating this important relationship for your protagonist? Often it's already suggested in the screenplay, only you haven't allowed it to flourish. To find it, go through the script and make a list of all the characters your hero comes into contact with. Who are they, how much do they affect the plot action, what do they have to offer your protagonist that increases his value in the story? One or more characters should come to the foreground. Now ask which of these characters would have the most at stake from a liaison with your protagonist? Then define what type of relationship it would be.

Once you've determined the relationship, you have to show it matters to your protagonist. To make it really dramatically productive, you want to be sure it will be affected by the conflict. This is key. Stress from the conflict must test this relationship: Will this challenge break it or make this connection even stronger? The conflict needs to threaten the ties, resulting in rising stakes that make the trouble more personal to the protagonist.

How much time you spend with this relationship depends on the project. In *Shakespeare in Love*, the central relationship between Will and Viola is really the whole story. In *Erin Brockovich*, Erin and George's relationship makes up a strong subplot to support the theme of a woman realizing her independence. It develops and is threatened by the conflict, which ultimately causes it to break. Part of the effectiveness of *Erin Brockovich* is in how we see Erin affecting others and being affected by them as well. This is the real power of the movie, and it is the real power of any movie.

Stories are best told in terms of relationships, which are matrices of emotions. If a character's pursuit of a goal affects no one, he won't affect the audience. He must relate to other characters, positively or negatively, to make a lasting impression.

Just as in our lives, relationships on-screen have meaning only to the extent they engage and arouse our emotions. We love or hate, care or feel disdain for someone; in drama, these emotions color the audience's reactions toward the characters.

Great writers—screenwriters, novelists, playwrights—understand that characters must react emotionally to each other to enable the audience to experience the power of the story. They create actions that are both logical and surprising to represent these emotional states and generate memorable plots. Readers and audiences not only see the character's nature rendered in their acts but glean his motivations, too.

In viewing a great film, the audience shares a wide range of emotions with the characters. It is the truth of this experience that keeps a film feeling timeless.

CHAPTER 10

IN THE END

Writing a screenplay is a daunting task, perhaps the hardest part of the filmmaking process. The screenwriter works alone most of the time and must be both artist and businessman. He must find what's true for his characters and story, then ask himself if it will all play in the current marketplace. He works on faith, usually without pay, hoping, believing, praying his story will captivate a succession of readers and make it to that point in the Hollywood food chain where, finally, there's a reader whose "yes" means a sale, even if the script is just optioned. Even then there are perilous waters to cross: Strong scripts that read well may still not inspire confidence about how they'll work on the screen. *American Beauty* and *Se7en* circulated around Hollywood for a number of years before producers and studios had the courage to produce them against the conventional wisdom. Each became a surprise hit.

William Goldman, Oscar-winning screenwriter and Hollywood sage, also authored the best-known adage about the Hollywood development process: "Nobody knows anything." He doesn't mean development people don't know how to do their jobs. Yes, there *are* people in the business who really don't know what they're doing (and damn it all, sometimes they have hits!). But many more creative people are working their hardest and pursuing their craft, whether it's screenwriting, producing, development, or production. Goldman means that picking a winner in the movie business is like horse racing; you can never find a sure bet. No one really knows what the audience wants. Who can predict if an idea over lunch, or a screenplay on paper, or an unreleased movie will become a hit? There are so many variables at each stage of development and production; and then there's the biggest unknown of all: what the audience wants at any particular moment.

What we do know is this: It all starts with a script. Filmmakers in Hollywood are *always* looking for a good script, the screenplay that excites them and will inspire others—producers, studios, and talent—to rally round and make a movie. Without a script, all we have are ideas. Everyone is full of ideas; it takes a writer to put them down on paper.

The great scripts are those that reach us emotionally. They create a flow of action we get caught up in and ride from beginning to end. The story is clear and understandable, whether it's *Wedding Crashers* or *Spartacus*. We always know what's going on, or we allow ourselves to be lulled into thinking we do so we can be "tricked" with a surprise twist at the climax of a "whodunit." Readers, development executives, and producers are all waiting for that story that will catch them up and carry them away. It doesn't have to be a special effects extravaganza. Look at *Rain Man*, *My Big Fat Greek Wedding*, or *The Pursuit of Happyness*. None of these films has any more special effects than an episode of *Ozzie and Harriet*, but each is beloved by legions of viewers. It's the story on the page with nothing more in the way of special effects than twelve-point black type that moves us.

"Nobody knows anything" in the way of predicting taste. But

we do know this: Successful movies always work at an emotional level. *The Art of Plotting* outlines ways to make your stories more emotionally compelling. The ideas are in your hands. But you're a writer, that's what makes you different from everyone else in Hollywood. They're all talkers.

And they can't do anything without your input. So take these ideas and use them in your writing. With hard work and good luck, they'll be talking about your scripts.

REFERENCED FILMS

Not every title on this list is a great film, but each one can teach you an aspect of screenwriting and filmmaking. As you delve into this art, you'll want to study as many different types of films as possible. Every genre has its own particular considerations with which you should be familiar.

If there's a film mentioned in this book you haven't seen, rent it. Almost all of them will be worth your time.

About Schmidt
Adaptation
African Queen, The
Amélie
American Beauty
Annie Hall
Apollo 13
As Good As It Gets
Best Years of Our Lives, The
Blair Witch Project, The
Break-Up, The
Bruce Almighty
Capote
Casablanca
Cast Away
Chinatown
Citizen Kane
City of God
Close Encounters of the Third Kind
D.O.A
Dangerous Liaisons
Déjà Vu
Departed, The
Devil Wears Prada, The
Die Hard
Diner
E.T.: The Extra-Terrestrial
Erin Brockovich
Field of Dreams
Five Easy Pieces
Forest Gump
Friday Night Lights
Fugitive, The
Gladiator
Good Girl, The
Good Will Hunting
Graduate, The
Groundhog Day
Grudge, The
Happy Endings
Harry Potter films
High Noon
His Girl Friday
Hours, The

House of Sand and Fog, The

I ❤ Huckabees

Invincible

It Happened One Night

James Bond films

Jaws

Jerry Maguire

Kill Bill, Vols. 1 and 2

Last of the Mohicans, The

Lawrence of Arabia

Liar, Liar

Little Children

Little Miss Sunshine

Lord of the Rings, The (trilogy)

Man Who Knew Too Much, The

Master and Commander

Matrix, The

Midnight Cowboy

Million Dollar Baby

Miracle

Monster

Monster's Ball

Moonstruck

Mr. & Mrs. Smith

Munich

My Best Friend's Wedding

My Big Fat Greek Wedding

Nashville

National Treasure

Nick of Time

North by Northwest

One Flew over the Cuckoo's Nest

Panic Room

Perfect Storm, The

Piano, The

Pirates of the Caribbean

Poltergeist

Pride and Prejudice

Pulp Fiction

Pursuit of Happyness, The

Quiz Show

Raiders of the Lost Ark

Rain Man

Rashômon

Reflections in a Golden Eye

Risky Business

Roman Holiday

Saving Private Ryan

Schindler's List

Se7en

Shakespeare in Love

Shawn of the Dead

Shawshank Redemption, The

Sideways

Signs

Spartacus

Spider-Man

Star Wars IV: A New Hope

Station Agent, The

Stranger than Fiction

Terminator, The

Thin Red Line, The

Titanic

Tootsie

Touching the Void

War of the Roses

Wedding Crashers

Witness

Wizard of Oz, The

BIBLIOGRAPHY

Aristotle. *Poetics*, translated by Richard Janko. Indianapolis, IN, and Cambridge, MA: Hackett, 1987.

Armer, Alan A. *Writing the Screenplay*. Blemont, CA: Wadsworth, 1993.

Blacker, Irwin R. *The Elements of Screenwriting*. New York: MacMillan, 1996.

Cowgill, Linda J. *Secrets of Screenplay Structure: How to Recognize and Emulate the Structural Frameworks of Great Films.* Los Angeles: Lone Eagle, 1999.

——*Writing Short Films: Structure and Content for Screenwriters.* Los Angeles: Lone Eagle, 2005.

Egri, Lajos. *The Art of Dramatic Writing*. New York: Simon & Schuster, 1972.

Howard, David, and Mabley, Edward. *The Tools of Screenwriting: A Writer's Guide to the Craft and Elements of a Screenplay.* New York: St. Martins, 1993.

Johnson, Lincoln F. *Film: Space, Time, Light and Sound*. New York: Holt, Rinehart and Winston, 1974.

Jung, C. G. *Psychological Types*, a revision by R. F. C. Hull of the translation by H. G. Baynes. Princeton, NJ: Princeton University Press, 1971.

Kazan, Elia. *A Life*. Cambridge, MA: De Capo Press, 1997.

King, Viki. *How to Write a Movie in 21 Days*. New York: HarperResource Quill, 2001.

Lawson, John Howard. *Theory and Technique of Playwriting and Screenwriting*. New York: Garland, 1985.

Lumet, Sidney. *Making Movies.* New York: Vintage, 1995.

Martell, William C. *The Secrets of Action Screenwriting*. Studio City, CA: First Strike Productions, 2000.

Mehring, Margaret. *The Screenplay: A Blend of Film Form and Content*. Boston: Focal Press, 1989.

McKee, Robert. *Story: Substance, Structure, Style, and the Principles of Screenwriting.* New York: HarperEntertainment, 1997.

Perret, Gene. *How to Write & Sell Your Sense of Humor.* Cincinnati, OH: Writer's Digest Books, 1989.

Seger, Linda. *Making a Good Script Great*. New York: Samuel French, 1994.

Shaw, Harry. *Concise Dictionary of Literary Terms*. New York: McGraw-Hill Paperbacks, 1976.

Stanislavski, Constantin. *The Actor Prepares*, translated by Elizabeth Reynolds Hapgood. New York: Theater Arts Books, 1948.

Wordplay website. http://www.wordplayer.com

INDEX

A

About Schmidt:
narration, 90
unity of opposites, 31
Action:
principles of, 41
sequences, 109–110
tools, 66–74
complications, 69–71
obstacles, 66–69
reversal, 71–74
Active protagonist, 168–169
Adaptation, narration in, 90
African Queen, The, tasks in, 159
Agent for change, 31–35
defined, 32
American Beauty, 15–16, 78–79
action line, 18
antagonist, 29, 67
character goals, 18
climax, 105–106
conflict in, 28–29
core conflict in, 170
deepened characterization, 121–122
fearful responses, 64
first act, 100–101
foreshadowing conflict, 63
dangerous props, 63
narration, 90
obligatory scene, 145
passive antagonist, 164
revelation in, 86
rising conflict in, 60
plot breakdown, 56–60
scene sequences, 110–111
second act, 102–104
segments, 108–111
suspense in, 131–132
tasks in, 159
third act, 104–105
tracked conflict, 154
unity of opposites, 30–31
American Beauty, character growth/change, 19
Analysis tools, 167–175
core conflict to serve as story spine, identifying, 169–171
key relationship(s) the audience roots for, 172–175
passive antagonist, discovering, 167–169
positive/negative scene values, identifying, 171–172
Annie Hall, 10
narration, 90
unity of opposites, 31
Antagonists, 27–28
as obstacles, 67
passive, 163–165
Anticipation, relationship between surprise and, 140–143
Apollo 13:
tasks in, 159
ticking clock in, 137
Arrangement of events, 9–10
Art of Dramatic Writing, The (Egri), 77
As Good As It Gets, visual information, 93
Audience, expectations of, 140–143

B

Ball, Alan, 15–16
Best Years of Our Lives, The:
antagonist, 67
deepened characterization, 124–125
Big clocks, 137–138
Big Fat Greek Wedding, antagonist, 67
Blair Witch Project, The, obstacles in, 68

Break-Up, The, 27
unity of opposites, 31
Bruce Almighty, 16

C

Capote, 35, 37
Casablanca, 173
agent for change, 32, 34
commitment of protagonist, 77
complications in, 71
fearful responses, 64
internal conflict, 68
passive antagonist, 167–168
revelation in, 86
rising conflict, 50
Catch Me If You Can:
midpoint climax in, 116–117
structurally effective choices and decisions in, 84
Causality, 10–11
Cause-and-effect scene relationships, 10–11, 43–50
complex, 47–50
simple, 45–47
Cause-and-effect scene sequences, 96–97
Character arc, 155–156
Character tools, 74–87
choices and reversals, 82–84
structurally effective, 84–85
conflict reveals character, 77–79
decisions/choices, 79–82
protagonists make commitments, 76–77
revelation, 85–87
Characterizations, deepening, 119–122
Characters:
in conflict, 26–29
desires, 13
emotional life, 12
emotional reactions, 14–16, 18
goal of, 41
growth/change, 19–21
provoking to take action, 168
roadblocks on hero's path, 21
Chekhov, Anton, 63
Chinatown:
complications in, 70–71
dialogue explaining character, 75
revelation in, 85–86
simple cause-and-effect scene relationships, 46–47
Choices, 79–82
defined, 79–80
and drama, 81
and reversals, 82–84
structurally effective, 84–85
Citizen Kane, 10
City of God, violence in, 35
Close Encounters of the Third Kind, decision/choice in, 81
Complex cause-and-effect scene relationships, 47–50
Complications, 18, 69–71, 101–102
defined, 69
unexpected, 70–71, 135–136
Conflict, 4–6, 11
agent for change, 31–35
characters in, 26–29
core, identifying, 169–171
emotional/physical, 35
evolution and consequences, purpose of, 24
foreshadowing, 61–64
importance vs. big, 36–37
insufficient amount of, 167–169
internal, 68
locking, 30–31
meaningful, 29–30
rising, 50–60
role of, 23–40, 40
and tension, 24–26
Core conflict:
defined, 170
identifying, 169–171

Crosscutting, 134–135
Crowe, Cameron, 75, 88, 172

D

Dangerous Liaisons, 10–11
Decisions, 79–82
  defined, 79
  and drama, 81
Departed, The, 7
Desire, 23
Devil Wears Prada, The, structurally effective choices and decisions in, 84–85
Die Hard:
  rising conflict, 60
  tasks in, 159
Diner, crosscutting in, 134–135, 141
D.O.A., ticking clock in, 137
Drama:
  compared to narrative prose, 5
  death in, 31
  obstacles as pivotal to, 66
  requirements of, 1–7
Dramatic conflict, *See* Conflict
Dubus III, Andre, 25

E

Elements of Screenwriting, The (Blacker), 12
Emotion, defined, 12
Emotional cues, 14
Emotional pattern of plot, 12–17
Emotional reactions, 14–16, 18
Erin Brockovich, 35
  audience information, 157–158
  character growth/change, 19–21
  complex cause-and-effect scene relationships, 48–49
  deepened characterization, 120, 123
  development of conflict in, 38–39
  obstacles in, 68
  plan of action, 89–90
  relationships in, 175
  simple cause-and-effect scene relationships, 45–46
E.T.: The Extra-Terrestrial:
  anticipation in, 141–142
  decision/choice in, 81
Events, outline, 97–98
Exposition tools, 87–93
  main exposition, 88–89
  minor conflicts, 92
  narration, 90–91
  plan of action, 89–90
  visual information, 92–93

F

Failure of protagonist, importance of, 39–40
Fearful responses, 64
Feature films, groups of scenes in, 98–99
Field of Dreams, 37
  narration, 90–91
Field, Syd, 65
Film, as temporal art form, 5–6
Film segments, *See* Segments
Fitzgerald, F. Scott, 114
Five Easy Pieces:
  choices/reversals in, 82–84
  passive antagonist, 164
Foreshadowing conflict, 61–64
  dangerous props, 63
  defined, 61
  fearful responses, 64
  in *Jaws*, 61
  showing the audience the trouble ahead, 62–63
  uncompromising characters, 61–62
Forrest Gump, 78
Friday Night Lights, preparation scene, 126
Fugitive, The:
  agent for change, 34

complications in, 70
crosscutting in, 134
giving the audience information in, 133–134
unexpected complications, 136

G

Genre:
and conflict, 140
expectations in, 140
Gladiator, violence in, 35
Goldman, William, 177–178
Good Girl, The:
complications in, 70
fearful responses, 64
structurally effective choices and decisions in, 84
Good Will Hunting, 37
Graduate, The, ticking clock in, 138
Grant, Susannah, 49
Groundhog Day, deepened characterization in, 122
Groups of scenes, 98–106
act one, 99–100
act two, 101–104
structural considerations, 99–100
Grudge, The, obstacles in, 68

H

Happy Endings, written cards, 91
Harry Potter films, relationships in, 174
High Noon, ticking clock in, 137
His Gal Friday, tasks in, 159
Hitchcock, Alfred, 132–133, 136
Hours, The, 35
narration, 90
House of Sand and Fog, The, 25

I

I ♥ Huckabees, 31
foreshadowing conflict, 62
Internal conflicts, 68
Invincible, preparation scene, 126
It Happened One Night, ticking clock in, 138

J

James Bond films, 29, 137
Jaws, 16–17
conflict in, 29
decision/choice in, 82
deepened characterization in, 122
foreshadowing conflict in, 61
obligatory scene, 144
obstacles in, 69
playing the beats in, 139
reversal in, 72–73
rising conflict in, 51
plot breakdown, 53–55
tracked conflict in, 152
Jerry Maguire, 15, 35
antagonist, 67, 172
commitment of protagonist, 77
conflict in, 28–29
dialogue explaining character, 75
main exposition, 88
narration, 90–91
obligatory scene, 144–145
plan of action, 89
preparations and consequences scenes, 130
revelation in, 86
Jeunet, Jean-Pierre, 149

K

Kill Bill, Vol. 1 and *Vol. 2*, 4
suspense in, 132

L

Last of the Mohicans, agent for change, 34
Laurant, Guillaume, 149

Lawrence of Arabia, consequence scene, 130
Liar, Liar, ticking clock in, 138
Linear plot construction, 10
Little Children, 26
  narration, 90
Lord of the Rings, The:
  fearful responses in, 64
  foreshadowing conflict in, 62–63
  violence in, 35

M

Main exposition, 88–89
  defined, 87–88
Making a Good Script Great (Seger), 100
Man Who Knew Too Much, The, unexpected complications in, 136
Master and Commander, segments, 107
Matrix, The:
  rising conflict, 60
  structurally effective choices and decisions in, 84
Meaning, development of, 6–7
Meaningful conflict, 29–30
Mendes, Sam, 15–16
Midnight Cowboy, relationships in, 174
Midpoint, 102
Million Dollar Baby, violence in, 35
Minor conflicts, 92
Minor reversal, 73
Miracle, preparation scene, 126
Monster, violence in, 35
Monster's Ball:
  core conflict, 170
  obligatory scene, 145–146
Moonstruck, 37
Mounting action, building a sense of, 49–50
Mr. & Mrs. Smith, unity of opposites, 30
Munich:
  commitment of protagonist, 77
  violence in, 35
My Best Friend's Wedding, ticking clock in, 138
My Big Fat Greek Wedding, 178

N

Narration, 90–91
Narrative films, 6
Nashville, 155
National Treasure, unity of opposites, 31
Nick of Time, ticking clock in, 137
Nonlinear plot construction, 10
North by Northwest:
  giving the audience information in, 133
  main exposition, 88
  revelation in, 86
  violence in, 35

O

Obligatory scene, 143–146
  tie to theme and conflict, 145
Obstacles, 18, 66–69
  type of, 66–67
Oedipus Rex, internal conflict, 68
One Flew over the Cuckoo's Nest, 25
  deepened characterization, 120–121
  obligatory scene, 144
  scene clock, 138
  scenes of preparation and consequence, 128–129
Opposing characters, 27
Opposites, unity of, 30–31
Ozzie and Harriet, 178

P

Panic Room, 29–30
Passive antagonist, 163–165
  discovering, 167–169
Perfect Storm, The:
  obstacles in, 67

trapped characters, 76
Physical obstructions, 67–68
Physical violence, 35
Piano, The:
agent for change, 32
narration, 90–91
uncompromising characters, 61–62
violence in, 35
Pirates of the Caribbean:
commitment of protagonist, 76
minor conflicts, 92
reversals in, 72
Plan of action, 89–90
Plot:
action/reaction and cause/effect, 49–50
arrangement of events, 9–10
causality, 10–11
conflict, 11
defined, 9–11, 11
emotional pattern of, 12–17
ordering of actions/emotions, 13–14
Plot action, logical progression of, 46
Plot construction, 147–165
audience understanding, anticipating, 160–162
character arc, 155–156
exposition, mishandling of, 156–158
keeping the story on track with a tasks, 158–160
overplotted action, 147–152
passive antagonist, 163–165
to-ing and fro-ing, 162–163
tracking, 152–155
Plot line, audience's anticipation of, 72
Plot spine, identifying core conflict to serve as, 169–171
Plot structure, 2
Plotting:
action tools, 66–74
character tools, 74–87
compared to structure, 113–114
for emotion vs. sentimentality, 122–125
exposition tools, 87–93
midpoint and act climaxes, 114–116
real art of, 113–146
segments, 98, 106–111
story sequence, 95–111
for suspense, 131–139
tools of, 65–93
Poltergeist, 68
Poseidon, ticking clock in, 137
Positive/negative scene values, identifying, 171–172
Preparations and consequences, 125–131
and audience experience, 130
defined, 126
development and outline of plot, 130–131
Pride and Prejudice, 35
Prometheus Bound, internal conflict, 68
Protagonist:
action of, 3–4
commitment made by, 76–77
and conflict, 4–6
reader's apathy for, 173
successes of, 39
Pulp Fiction, 10
decision/choice in, 81–82
tasks in, 159
Pursuit of Happyness, The, 178

Q

Quiz Show:
reversal in, 74
structurally effective choices and decisions in, 84

R

Raiders of the Lost Arc, unity of opposites, 30
Rain Man, 35, 37, 178
core conflict, 170

foreshadowing conflict, 62
relationships in, 174
Rashômon, 10
Reflections in a Golden Eye, 10–11
Relationships, 172–175
Revelation, 85–87
consequences of, 87
Reversal, 71–74
and choices, 82–84
structurally effective, 84–85
defined, 71
leading to a reverse in the direction of the plot action, 87
major/minor, 72
Rising conflict, 50–60
defined, 50
Risky Business:
agent for change, 34
anticipation in, 143
minor conflicts, 92
protagonist's successes, 39
reversal in, 73
Roman Holiday, structurally effective choices and decisions in, 85

S

Sarcey, Francisque, anticipation in, 143–144
Saving Private Ryan, preparation scene, 126–127
Scene clocks, 138
Scene relationships:
cause-and-effect, 43–50
foreshadowing conflict, 61–64
rising conflict, 50–60
types of, 42
Scene sequence, 109–111
and scope of main conflict, 111
Schindler's List, 15
Screenwriting:
action, 5–6, 23, 77, 142
anticipation, 140–143
causal relationships, 42–43
cause-and-effect scene relationships, 43–50
character tools, 74–87
characters, 18, 63, 78, 119–122, 169, 175
choices and reversals, 82–84
conflict, 11, 23–26, 31, 36–38, 141
and reversals, 82–84
decisions/choices, 79–82
emotion, 122–125
emotion in screenplay, xii, 12–15, 17, 21
essential ingredients, 3–7
exposition tools, 87–93
externalizing characters' feelings/thoughts, 6
main exposition, 88–89
managing the emotions of your audience, xi
midpoint and act climaxes, 114–119
minor conflicts, 92–93
narration, 90–91
old rule of, 44
overplotting, xii–xiii
plan, 89–90
preparations and consequences scenes, 125–131
process, 114
and requirements of a film story, x
revelation, 85–87
reversal, 71–74
structurally effective choices and decisions, 84–85
subplot, 31–32
suspense, plotting for, 131–139
tension and meaning, 5
theme, development of, 6
and underlying principle of drama, 2–3
Se7en, 25
act one, 100–101
act three, 104

act two, 102
action sequence, 110
agent for change, 32–34
conflict in, 28–30
foreshadowing conflict, 64
preparation scene, 127–128
scene sequence, 110
segments, 107–108
suspense in, 131–132
tasks in, 159
tracked conflict, 154
violence in, 35
Seger, Linda, 65–66
Segments, 98, 106–111
American Beauty, 108–111
defined, 106–107
Se7en, 107–108
Shakespeare in Love, 18
anticipation in, 142–143
character arc, 155–156
character growth/change, 19
final climax in, 118
midpoint climax in, 117–118
minor conflicts, 92
tracked conflict, 152–153, 155
visual information, 92
written card, 91
Shawn of the Dead, trapped characters, 76
Shawshank Redemption, The, 4
Sideways, 37
Signs, foreshadowing conflict, 61
Simple cause-and-effect scene relationships, 45–47
Spartacus, 178
Spider-Man:
decisions/choices, 80–81
deepened characterization, 122
rising conflict in, 60
visual information, 92
Spine, *See* Core conflict
Star Wars IV: A New Hope, 27
written card, 91
Station Agent, The, passive antagonist, 164, 168
Story lines, 17–21
characters caught in conflict, 78
Story, plot structure of, 2–3
Story points, 96
Story sequence, 95–111
events, outline of, 97–98
Story spine, identifying core conflict to serve as, 169–171
Stranger than Fiction, 4, 26
agent for change, 34–35
narration, 90
suspense in, 132
ticking clock in, 137
Structurally effective choices and reversals, 84–85
Suspense:
giving the audience information, 132–133
playing the beats, 139
plotting for, 131–139
tension compared to, 131
ticking clock, 137–138
unexpected complications, 135–136

T

Tension, 35
and conflict, 24–26
forms of, 25–26
increasing, 51–52
of mystery, 26
of relationships, 25–26
of surprise, 26
of the task, 25
Terminator, The, ticking clock in, 137
Thin Red Line, The, 126
Three Requirements of Drama, 3–7
Ticking clock, 137–138
Titanic:
obstacles in, 67–68
trapped characters, 76

Tootsie, 37
  minor conflicts, 92
  protagonist's successes, 39
Touching the Void, 26
Towne, Robert, 165
Tracking:
  character arc, 155–156
  conflict, 152–154
  exposition, 156–158
Twists, plotting, 73

U

Unexpected complications, 135–136
Unity of opposites, 30–31

V

Visual information, 92–93

W

War of the Roses, 31
Wedding Crashers, 178
  protagonist's successes, 39
  rising conflict, 60
Witness:
  action sequence, 110
  agent for change, 32
  complications in, 71
  obstacles in, 68–69
  revelation in, 87
Wizard of Oz, The, 26
  obstacles in, 69
  tasks in, 158
Written cards, 91

ABOUT THE AUTHOR

Linda J. Cowgill, author of *Writing Short Films* and *Secrets of Screenplay Structure*, currently heads the screenwriting department at the Los Angeles Film School. She has written for film and television, and taught at the American Film Institute, Loyola Marymount University, and the Boston Film Institute. She has presented *The Art of Plotting* seminar in Los Angeles, New York, and Miami.